How Do I Teach RE?
2nd Edition

THE WESTHILL PROJECT RE 5–16 is a comprehensive range of materials for teaching Religious Education in schools, from lower primary to upper secondary level.

In addition to this project manual, *How Do I Teach RE?*, materials are available as follows:

Christianity	**Islam**	**Judaism**	
Christians 1	*Muslims 1*	*Jews 1*	*(lower primary)*
Christians 2	*Muslims 2*	*Jews 2*	*(upper primary)*
Christians 3	*Muslims 3*	*Jews 3*	*(lower secondary)*
Christians 4	*Muslims 4*	*Jews 4*	*(upper secondary*

Christians Photopack   *Muslims Photopack*   *Jews Photopack*
(20 colour photographs in A3 format with background information)

Teacher's Manual   *Teacher's Manual*   *Teacher's Manual*
(comprehensive overview of each world religion and specific teaching guidelines)

Three resource packs are also available for primary RE:

Life Themes in the Early Years
Pack 1 The Natural World, Celebrations
Pack 2 Stages of Life, Lifestyles
Pack 3 Relationships, Rules and Issues
(40 large format illustrations and photographs with a Teacher's Manual)

Further materials are in preparation consisting of Life Themes materials for Key Stage 3 and photopacks.

THE WESTHILL PROJECT RE 5–16

How Do I Teach RE?
2nd Edition

Garth Read
John Rudge
Geoff Teece
Roger B Howarth

Stanley Thornes (Publishers) Ltd

First published by Mary Glasgow Publications Limited 1986
Reprinted with corrections 1988

Second edition first published in 1992 by:
Stanley Thornes (Publishers) Ltd
Old Station Drive
Leckhampton
CHELTENHAM GL53 0DN
England

A catalogue record for this book is available from the British library.

ISBN 0–7487–1470–7

Typeset by Tech-Set, Gateshead, Tyne & Wear
Printed and bound in Great Britain at The Bath Press, Avon

Contents

Acknowledgements

How do I Teach RE? was first published in 1986 as the main project manual of the Westhill Project RE 5–16. It arose out of many years of dialogue with colleagues working in the field of Religious Education. The project has been developed by the staff of the Regional RE Centre (Midlands), Westhill College, Birmingham, in collaboration with practising teachers and members of the various religious communities.

Geoff Teece, John Rudge and Margaret Breiner, in consultation with Garth Read and many other colleagues, have produced this revised, updated version. The three-circle model of the RE field of enquiry which lies at the heart of this book remains unchanged. This model had its genesis in work done in the Regional RE Centre (Midlands) by Garth Read and Michael Grimmitt in 1975. Garth Read then shared this model with the Religious Education Curriculum Project Team of which he was a member, working in the Department of Education, Queensland, Australia. The Australian team published the model in a slightly amended form in 1977. The Queensland RECP team has given us permission to include in the manual some material which was developed during the time that Garth Read was with them. For this we are most grateful. We also thank the Department of Education, Queensland, for permission to use the material on spirituality, pages 13–16.

Foreword to the second edition

Westhill College began out of the most unlikely of campaigns. George Hamilton Archibald, a migrant from North America, founded it with the help of the Cadbury family to promote graded Sunday School lessons. In 1907 this was revolutionary. He argued that religion was the most educational of subjects when it was the food by which a child grew: it was not educational at all when it was turned into the abstraction of theological dogmas. In this he shared the outlook of his compatriot, William James, author of the classic work, *The Variety of Religious Experience.*

The first book ever written at Westhill was the aptly named *The Child in the Midst.* We pioneered child-centred learning here. It made us non-conformist then; it may come to do so again. *How do I Teach RE?* continues this tradition. Its first edition has proved very popular with teachers and has established a broad view of RE which remains very influential despite attacks on it from narrower perspectives.

This second edition incorporates much new thinking about the curriculum which has developed with the passing of the 1988 Education Reform Act. It recognises the enormous amount of work on attainment and assessment done in the Westhill RE Centre and elsewhere. At the same time, it maintains a continuity of approach from the past. 'History', commented Ted Hughes, 'is only as old as the latest newborn child.' There is no end to the age-old quest for life to be richly meaningful. That is what this book is about; we believe that it is also what education ultimately is all about. It encourages tolerance, but the deepest tolerance comes as a by-product of searching for truth together, not from evading it. Tolerance is never an end in itself. The quest never ends. It must be renewed for each generation. This new edition is part of that process.

Jack Priestley
Westhill College
Selly Oak
Birmingham
July, 1992

General introduction

The Westhill Project RE 5–16 is a comprehensive range of materials for teaching Religious Education in schools, from lower primary to upper secondary level. It provides an educational approach to the subject of RE in a multicultural society, devised with both the specialist and non-specialist teacher in mind. The materials are carefully graded to offer a clear developmental structure through the 5–16 age range. They are nonetheless designed to be used flexibly; all the components, while interrelated, can be used independently.

The range of materials

The main project manual *How do I Teach RE?* explores RE as a school subject and shows how its aims can be translated into classroom practice, providing clear guidelines on syllabus planning and school programme development.

The consequences for RE of the new legislation outlined in the 1988 Education Reform Act are dealt with in some detail in this new edition. In particular, the revision of the sections 'Concepts, Attitudes, Skills and Knowledge in RE' and 'How can RE be assessed?' reflect the developments that have taken place in these two important areas since 1988.

These two new chapters draw heavily on a recent publication, *Assessing, Recording and Reporting RE*, Regional RE Centre (Midlands), 1991. Other parts of the text have been revised in order to reflect the continuing process of critical appraisal of the work of the Centre.

The materials for three of the major world religions – Christianity, Islam and Judaism – are available in the following format:

- **Teacher's manual** A comprehensive overview of the religion and specific teaching guidelines.

- **Photopack** 20 coloured photographs in A3 format, with detailed information on the back which 1) describes the content of the photograph, 2) explores its significance to the faith, and 3) outlines the beliefs reflected by the content of the photograph.

- **Four fully illustrated Pupils' Books**
  Book 1 Key Stage 1 (lower primary)
  Book 2 Key Stage 2 (upper primary)
  Book 3 Key Stage 3 (lower secondary)
  Book 4 Key Stage 4 (upper secondary)

A photopack for Hinduism (accompanied by detailed notes for the teacher) is planned for publication in 1992. Photopacks for Sikhism and Buddhism are being planned for later publication.

A separate strand of life themes completes the project. Three resource packs for the early years, each with a practical Teacher's manual, have already been published, and Pupils' books and Teacher's manuals for life themes at Key Stages 2 and 3 are currently being prepared.

PART ONE

What is RE trying to achieve?

This is essentially a practical book, setting out to show how a general aim for RE may be translated in a consistent way into lessons in the classroom.

It may seem presumptuous – even somewhat dogmatic – to begin with such a bald statement, as though the answer to the question 'What is RE trying to achieve?' is indisputable. That is not the intention. The purpose in stating this aim here is simply to declare, right at the outset, the kind of RE that this manual is promoting. It is not to suggest that this is the only way of stating the aim of RE, nor to deny that there are other views of the subject, some of which might conflict with the view taken here.

The debate about the nature and aims of the school subject 'RE' has been going on for a long time. Teachers who wish to explore this debate, and the way in which thinking about the subject has changed in recent years, may like to refer to some of the books and articles listed in the select bibliography. This manual makes no attempt to enter into this general debate. It does, however, seek to reflect, in practical terms, the most recent thinking about the subject, particularly the kind of developments which find expression in a whole range of new local authority agreed syllabuses.

The agreed syllabus remains the legal basis for the type of RE that is taught in county schools in England and Wales. This basis is derived from the 1944 Education Act and has been reaffirmed with the 1988 Education Reform Act. The wording of the 1988 Act recognises the developments that have taken place in the subject since 1944. In particular, the 1988 Act requires that any new agreed syllabus must 'reflect the fact that the religious traditions in Great Britain are in the main Christian whilst taking account of the teachings and practices of the other principal religious traditions represented in Great Britain.' It is now firmly established that agreed syllabuses should reflect the multifaith nature of society whilst giving due regard to the position and influence of the Christian tradition. Therefore, although expressed in different ways, the 1988 Act and recent agreed syllabuses share a broadly common thinking about the subject and embody principles similar to those underlying this manual.

These recent developments in the theory of the subject have not always been complemented by parallel developments in curriculum and classroom practice. Before considering this issue, however, it is only right that the general principles on which this manual is based should be made clear. Here they are stated briefly, with some explanations where necessary, but no attempt is made to argue the case for them in detail. It is hoped that this statement of principles will shed some light on the ways in which the subject is developed.

The aim and general principles of Religious Education

AIM OF RE	The principal aim of Religious Education is to help children mature in relation to their own patterns of belief and behaviour through exploring religious beliefs and practices and related human experiences.
PRINCIPLES OF RE	1 Children need to develop their own beliefs and values and a consistent pattern of behaviour.
	2 RE has a particularly important contribution to make to spiritual, moral and social development of children.
	3 In RE, the role of the teacher is that of educator.
	4 As in all other subject areas, the teaching of RE must be related to the ages and abilities of the children being taught.
	5 RE will help children to explore a range of religious beliefs and practices and related human experiences.
	6 RE has a major contribution to make in helping children to develop a positive and understanding attitude towards diversity in our pluralistic society.
	7 RE does not make assumptions about, or preconditions for, the personal commitments of teachers or children.

Figure 1 Aim and principles of RE

1 Children need to develop their own beliefs and values and a consistent pattern of behaviour

It is a basic assumption of RE that the simple fact of being human confronts us every day with experiences, situations and events to which we have to make responses. The particular responses we make will vary according to a number of factors. One of the most important of these is the complex of attitudes and beliefs which go to make our system of values and outlook on life.

Our beliefs and attitudes, and the kind of behaviour and style of life through which we express them, have in turn been informed and shaped by a variety of influences. Some people will, at an early stage in their lives, acquire or adopt a pattern of belief and behaviour which will remain largely unchanged over the years. Others will be continually assessing, reforming and sometimes changing altogether their system of values and outlook on life. Of course, not everyone will spend their every waking moment wrestling with these issues. Some may appear to give hardly any thought to them. Some may regard them as irrelevant in the light of pressing practical considerations. The capacity to think about them or act upon their responses to them may not be developed to the same extent in all

people; and many may find it hard to articulate their views or explain their actions. All human beings are, nevertheless, inevitably involved in acquiring and developing attitudes and behaviour patterns – that is part of what is involved in being human.

Having beliefs and acting upon them is one of the most important humanising factors. This is particularly true when people find themselves in a situation where they are forced to make a choice between two alternatives. Some may respond simply on the basis of their own self-interest and initial feelings. Others, however, may choose the less attractive alternative, at whatever personal cost, because it squares with their values and expresses their beliefs. By doing so, they rise above merely instinctive responses, and illustrate their capacity for being genuinely human.

It is also part of being human that we take responsibility for our beliefs and actions and embrace them as our own. This element of responsibility is an important aspect of maturity. It follows that mature human beings will think responsibly about their beliefs and will act upon them in a responsible manner. Here, a distinction can be drawn. On the one hand there are people who simply adhere to beliefs and customs out of habit or because they have inherited them or been indoctrinated into them. On the other hand, some people have reflected upon them, proved them on the test-bed of their own experiences and subjected them to the scrutiny of the beliefs and values of others.

2 RE has a particularly important contribution to make to the spiritual, moral and social development of children

RE is, of course, not the only contributor to the spiritual, moral and social development of children. This takes place in a whole range of contexts of which school is only one and probably not the most important or influential. Family life and parental guidance undoubtedly shape the lives of children, often in subconscious yet profound ways. All kinds of groups – local, religious or interest based – are also influential, as is the particular peer group to which children belong. Children's own experiences will also be a forceful tutor in shaping their outlook, values and commitments. Most of these learning experiences and situations will be found outside school and will continue well beyond school.

Schools do, however, have an essential role to play in this aspect of development. They provide an educational context in which it may take place. There is no one school subject to which it is confined, least of all a subject called 'Personal and Social Education.' All subjects contribute, as does the hidden or informal curriculum. The general ethos of the school and the values it represents have an important part to play, and all teachers have a contribution to make.

Moreover, the area of spiritual, moral and social education is important for all children in school. It should not be reserved for the so-called less able. The notion that those of greater ability are too academically orientated to have time for it is evidence of confused educational priorities. As children mature, it is important that they assume responsibility for themselves and for their own actions, that they act in a responsible way towards each other and that they are given the opportunity to reflect on the important spiritual and moral questions they will encounter. It is in this area that RE has a large contribution to make.

3 In RE the role of the teacher is that of educator

As the understanding of the place of RE in the school curriculum has changed over the years, so also has the understanding of the role of the teacher of RE.

As an educator, the teacher of RE will be concerned to encourage and promote an open, critical and sympathetic approach to the subject. This implies that the teacher will require just those qualities in his or her approach. It is an approach based on a willingness to enquire and to raise questions without necessarily arriving at firm and conclusive answers. At the same time it requires a commitment to the value and importance of the enquiry, and a conviction that it is worthwhile for the teacher as well as the children.

In this approach there will be no question of imposing the values and beliefs of any particular religion on children. However, the teacher of RE will be concerned to support beliefs such as the value of human life in all its diversity by encouraging attitudes of sensitivity, respect, open-mindedness and empathy in children.

More specifically, teachers of RE will be concerned to stimulate interest in the various ways in which beliefs shape and influence people's lives. They will involve children in widening their horizons and deepening their perceptions about the world around them, and will encourage them to reflect on their own outlook.

The teacher of RE, therefore, has to tread a difficult path, surrounded by pitfalls. The two most dangerous of these are the one that pushes the subject back towards the instructional model, and the one that removes all elements of controversy from the subject, thus robbing it of its essential relevance. The task of the teacher of this subject calls for the highest professional skills if RE is not to degenerate to the level where it becomes an easy target for its detractors.

4 As in all other subject areas, the teaching of RE must be related to the ages and abilities of the children being taught

This educational principle is firmly established as part of the essential understanding which teachers bring to their task. This has not always been the case, and the implications of it have not always been applied in the classroom.

Extensive research in the areas of the cognitive and moral development of children has led to a recognition that adult categories, concepts and attitudes are in many cases quite foreign to a child's perception of things. At one time, the thinking in this area tended to suggest that the stages of children's development could be defined fairly clearly and that some kind of linear progression could be observed. More recent thinking has come to recognise the complexity in the process of development. Nonetheless, acknowledgement of the basic stages of children's educational and moral development has become part of the received wisdom of educational theory. It has important implications for the way in which RE is taught in schools.

In some areas of the curriculum it is possible to see development in children as taking place by the acquisition of concepts which gradually become more sophisticated. There is a sense in which children need to acquire one particular concept or skill before they can progress to the next. Development of understanding in RE takes place in a more subtle and less clearly definable way. That is partly because some of the ideas and concepts which children will come across in RE are, by their very nature, imprecise and open to many interpretations and responses. At the same time, when teaching RE teachers ought not to fall into the trap of assuming that children cannot grasp some of these concepts.

For this reason teachers at both primary and secondary levels need to have a clear grasp of the essential way in which the subject operates and the ways in which its objectives may be achieved. It is these things which this manual sets out to provide.

5 RE will help children to explore a range of religious beliefs and practices and related human experiences

The aim of the subject also encompasses its main areas of essential content which distinguish it from other subject areas. This is not to suggest that the only difference between RE and other subjects is the content or area of knowledge it deals with. It is rather to emphasise the importance of the exploration of the subject's content, or field of enquiry, as the means through which the subject's aim is to be realised.

RE in fact draws its content from three main areas which are discussed in Part 2. It is inevitable that one of these will deal with particular expressions of belief and practice, especially those enshrined in the great traditional belief systems which are a fundamental part of our human heritage and contemporary life. The exploration of these systems is an essential part of RE though not by any means the whole of it. Our model and method for such explorations is set out in Part Two.

It is not the intention here to enter into a discussion about the nature of religion. Definitions of religion are notoriously inadequate, however much light they may throw on some aspects of its nature. In RE we are concerned with the more practical question of how children are to make sense of the many ways in which they will encounter religious (and non-religious) belief and practice in their daily lives – in the media, in their local communities or among their friends. The focus is therefore on religion as a living and contemporary aspect of life, rather than as a subject for purely historical study.

Children will inevitably observe around them some of the great diversity of beliefs and commitments by which people live. This variety and diversity is important in RE. It is desirable that children should understand that matters of belief are often controversial and represent different outlooks and interpretations of human experience. Accurate information and thoughtful understanding in this area are far more preferable than slogans and propaganda.

Younger children will usually come to explore beliefs and values by observing the way people behave. RE, however, is not merely a study of the outward forms of religion. It will be concerned with exploring the feelings and attitudes that lie behind the behaviour, and with helping children to appreciate the importance in religion of drama, music, story and symbol, and of the way in which language is used figuratively to express meaning.

In the light of this, the view taken in this manual is that RE must include the consideration of different religious and non-religious views and traditions. This emphasis on diversity arises both from the nature of the subject and from the way in which it is to be taught.

This understanding is to be distinguished sharply from the view sometimes referred to as 'market place religion' – the idea that children are given an objective description of a variety of religions and then encouraged to choose one for themselves. This view is wholly unrealistic and shows no regard for either the desirability or the possibility of such choices, or to the ways in which particular commitments are made.

The exploration of religions is, however, only one aspect of RE, and the subject is not to be limited simply to the study of religion as a detached, academic exercise. RE will only be effective if this exploration of religion is related both to wider human experiences and issues and to the children's own outlooks.

The concern of RE with these wider areas is not merely peripheral to the subject but an essential element of it. The recognition of this was probably motivated at first by a desire to make the subject more relevant to the needs and interests of children. Indeed, attempts were made at one stage to demonstrate how an exploration of human experience in depth may lead to religious conclusions. That is not the view taken here. The approach of this manual is to recognise that there is an interrelationship between religion and a range of significant human experiences. An exploration of these related experiences will help children towards a better perception of the religious dimension, and will provide a broader background for informing and developing their own ideas and values. Indeed, we would want to stress that it is only through an exploration of all three areas (religious beliefs and practices, wider human experiences, and children's own outlooks), and of the relationships between them, that the aim of RE can be achieved.

6 RE has a major contribution to make in helping children to develop a positive and understanding attitude towards diversity in our pluralistic society

The sixth principle set out here is complementary to the second, but needs to be stated in its own right because of its importance. It stems from the kind of society which forms the context in which RE is taught as well as from the principles of the subject itself.

There is a serious, continuing debate about the kind of society in which our children are growing up. It arises partly from social fragmentation, partly from regional and cultural diversity and partly from the absence of any one over-arching set of values to which all or even most subscribe. Some view this as a grave defect, and there have been various attempts to impose or, at least, encourage some uniformity. Others see it as a saving grace. It has, however, been widely accepted in theory, if not entirely in practice, that the multicultural and pluralist nature of our society is a welcome and desirable benefit. As such it is a reflection of the shrinking and inter-dependent world in which we live, and in which 'we must learn to live together as brothers (and sisters!) or we shall perish as fools'. Schools have a part to play in encouraging an understanding of and positive attitude to this kind of pluralistic society.

RE, with its focus on questions of belief and value, attitude and outlook, behaviour and practice has a major contribution to make in this direction. Along with other subjects, and with the values represented by the school as a whole, RE contributes to the development of attitudes which promote and support a harmonious and tolerant society. An essential part of this development is an awareness of, and respect for, the beliefs and ways of life of people whose cultural background and traditions differ from those with which we may be familiar.

The concern for helping children to develop a positive, understanding and appreciative attitude towards diversity is closely related to the aims and content of RE. On the one hand, an attitude based on openness implies a readiness to explore the views of others in a way that emphasises accurate understanding. On the other hand, while seeking to avoid conflict (usually based on prejudice, misinformation, propaganda and aggression), it does encourage a frank exchange of views and experiences based on mutual respect and clarity. Openness in the context of RE does not imply a watering down or levelling process through which differences are disregarded, convictions and commitments left unexpressed. It does not mean that the essential challenge of the subject is reduced to the notion that 'all religions amount to the same thing'. It does, however, mean the encouragement of the exploration of differences in a way which does genuine justice to their distinctiveness in an atmosphere of open enquiry.

Clearly the potential for a well balanced and broadly based RE programme is usually much greater in areas and schools where cultural and religious diversity is present at first hand. It must nevertheless be understood that the nature of the subject – and of religion itself – implies that multifaith RE is as necessary in culturally mono-chrome areas as it is in areas of great diversity.

It must also be recognised that many children in county schools will probably have no clearly defined religious background, affiliation or commitment. RE cannot begin with any pre-suppositions about their commitments. The absence of traditional commitments reflects the secular (and often urban) aspect of our society. It is at least partly on account of this secular context that religious freedom and tolerance are promoted. There is no intention, as some have asserted, of narrowing children's outlook to a purely secular view of reality. Rather, in appreciating the pluralistic nature of religion, children may develop a considerably enriched outlook on life.

It is also important to recognise that, while society in Britain today may justifiably be described as both pluralistic and secular, it is the religion of Christianity that has played a major role in shaping and informing many of our cultural values and institutions. This recognition of the place and influence of Christianity in Britain means that its beliefs and practices should comprise an essential element of any RE programme. This point is, of course, highlighted in the 1988 Education Reform Act.

The prominence given to Christianity must, however, still be contained within a multifaith and multicultural context. There can be no question of religious or cultural superiority within the framework of RE, and Christianity itself, along with all other traditions, needs to be viewed in the light of its own diversity of belief and practice, which is very considerable.

7 RE does not make assumptions about, or preconditions for, the personal commitments of teachers or children

We recognise that there is a genuine problem about the way in which RE teachers may make their contribution to the spiritual, moral and social development of children. At face value the implications of the subject title 'Religious Education' appear to be both contradictory and undesirable. Unease about these implications is often exacerbated in the minds of some parents and teachers by their own experiences of RE when they were at school.

Criticisms of RE usually focus on the inter-pretations that are to be placed on 'Religious' and 'Education', and may come from opposite directions – some feeling that anything to do with religion undermines education and others holding that education undermines what religion is all about. In this manual we take the view that an equal emphasis can be placed on both – 'religious' in that we are dealing with an under-standing of religion in its widest sense, and 'education' in that the exercise takes place in an educational context and conforms with educational criteria.

The first of the criticisms is really concerned with the commitments of teachers of RE. There is an assumption that since religion is about commitment, teachers of RE will want to pass on their own views to children with the danger that they may indoctrinate them.

It is inevitable that teachers of RE, like all other teachers, will have their own particular commit-ment to a set of beliefs and values. These commit-ments will differ very widely from teacher to teacher.

There is certainly no one single set of beliefs with which they will all conform, and some will not be committed to any religious tradition. It is likely, however, that all teachers of RE will have some sort of deeply held convictions and beliefs.

It is quite clear that teachers of RE must not seek, either implicitly or explicitly, to indoctrinate children into their own particular outlook. At the same time they will use their professional expertise to make their views available in the classroom for children to explore in an educational context. Indeed, the teacher may well be one of the primary resources for helping children to understand the importance of commitment to beliefs and values. But teachers must tread a careful middle way between the dangers of trying to force their own views on children and the pitfalls of attempting to be so detached that children conclude that the whole exercise is academic and irrelevant.

What is certain is that without a belief in the value of the subject's aim, it will be extremely difficult to be a successful teacher of RE. This means that teachers must be committed to the importance of being clear, thoughtful and consistent in their own set of beliefs, values and attitudes, and of encouraging children to engage in the same task.

The second criticism arises from a concern that since RE is an educational activity, it might actually be undermining the commitment of children who are being nurtured at home or elsewhere in a particular religious tradition. This view implies that beliefs and values which are regarded as absolute in a faith community become merely relative in the context of RE in schools. If RE does not reinforce cultural and religious norms – so the argument runs – it cannot have any value.

In an educational context the absolute status of beliefs and values for those who hold them is both recognised and respected. Far from undermining children's commitments, RE should help them to think more clearly and deeply about them. At the same time, there is no question of assuming that one expression of commitment has greater universal validity than another. Children will certainly be encouraged to see their own commitment in the light of other people's commitments, but with a view to mutual respect rather than mutual destruction. They will also without doubt learn from and reflect on the views of others. It is not, however, the task of RE to determine beforehand what the outcome of their learning and reflection might be. It is the task of RE, to ensure that children have gained some understanding of religion by the time they leave school; that they have explored something of the relationship between religious perspectives and wider human experiences; and that they have reflected for themselves on the relevance of these perspectives and experiences for their own beliefs, attitudes and behaviour. The success of the subject can only be measured in the long term by the extent to which the exploration and reflection are continued beyond school into adult life.

PART TWO

What can be taught in RE?

Readers ought, at this point, to be reminded of the principal aim of Religious Education with which this manual began:

> Religious Education helps children mature in relation to their *own patterns of belief and behaviour* through exploring *religious beliefs and practices* and related *human experiences*.

The most significant phrases in this aim have now been highlighted because they indicate the three main areas from which religious education in schools draws its content. These three areas can be more easily represented through the diagram of the RE field of enquiry, shown below.

The field of enquiry provides an indication of the potential content which is suitable for use in RE in schools. The use of arrows in the diagram indicates that the three areas – traditional belief systems, shared human experience and individual patterns of belief – are intended to relate very closely to each other.

This Part of the manual concentrates on:

1 The three main areas of content in RE, and the criteria for selecting themes or topics from the field of enquiry.
2 The concepts, attitudes, skills and knowledge that can be developed through RE.

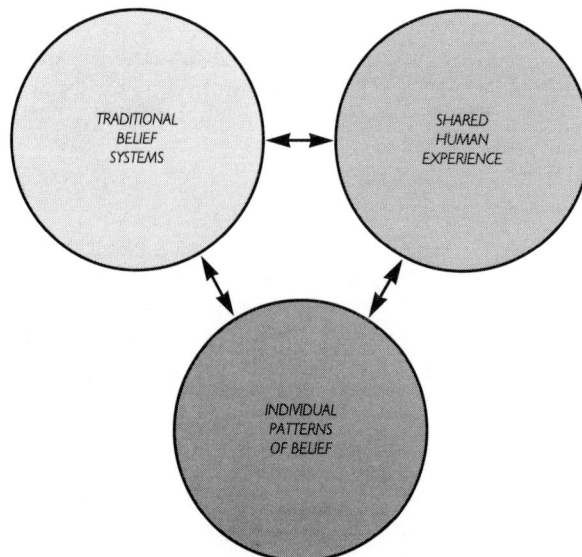

Figure 2 The RE field of enquiry

I The three main areas of content

Traditional belief systems

The world in which children are growing up today embraces a great variety of ideas and beliefs. Improved communications and the growth of the participation of ethnic minorities in society have made us increasingly aware of just how varied these ideas and beliefs are and how widely they range. Beliefs about the meaning and goal of life, about human nature and destiny, about what is right or wrong, about the origins of the world and the place of human beings in it – all these in one way or another influence the lives of people and the shape of cultures. With them are closely linked an equally varied range of outlooks, values, attitudes, styles of life and codes of conduct which give expression to them.

All these beliefs and ways of life are potential material for RE. There are, however, both theoretical and practical reasons for trying to narrow down this wide field to more manageable proportions. That is why it is more appropriate in RE to focus attention on those beliefs and practices which are widely shared and influential in the modern world. These are the beliefs and practices which form part of coherent systems or world views, and which we refer to here as *traditional belief systems*.

At this point it is important to guard against giving false impressions. There is a sense in which the notion of a traditional belief system can be misleading. The great religions of the world are, as a rule, far from systematic and do not fit easily into categories. They are much more akin to living and moving organisms, changing and developing, responding to situations, manifested in many colours, varieties and forms. Attempts to define, analyse and dissect them into their component parts does, in one sense, destroy their living wholeness and thus their essential nature. Nevertheless, the task of education does demand that we make use of models for exploration. In the case of young children in particular, the sense of the vibrant whole can

only be built up from a developing understanding of the constituent parts.

In using the term 'traditional belief system' we are not therefore trying to rob the reality of its living essence, but to point to the need for a suitable model that is both true to the nature of the reality and serves the educational task.

What is meant by 'systems'?

The fact that beliefs are widely shared, and hold together, however loosely, to give a kind of total response to the world, suggests that they may properly be referred to as systems. They are not, of course, rigid formulae, precisely structured or expressed in internally logical statements with inflexible codes of conduct and practice. Within these systems we undoubtedly find wide variations of interpretation, outlook and behaviour. Yet each one does hold together by some common bond and provides a distinctive worldview with which particular people and groups identify.

What is meant by 'traditional'?

Some of these systems have been more durable and pervasive than others. Some have had, and continue to have, a considerable influence over the lives of many millions of people. They form part of the rich heritage of ideas and sources of inspiration which shape great cultures. We therefore refer to them as traditional. Again, this is not to imply that they are merely museum pieces of historical interest, part of a bygone age, but that their influence has not been ephemeral, a mere passing shadow. Not only do they have a history of their own, they also continue to inspire and to command the commitment of people today. Their influence is living and vibrant.

What is meant by 'belief'?

We also refer to them as belief systems. This suggests that, from one point of view at least, they encompass a coherent view and focus upon a distinctive interpretation of life and of the world we live in. It does not, of course, imply that the only way in which these systems may be viewed is as a vehicle for providing clearly defined beliefs. Nor does it mean that there are not many other aspects which adherents may see as equally – or more – important. It is simply to recognise the way in which shared beliefs do influence and inform a range of attitudes and practice and provide a recognisable point of focus and identity, particularly for teaching purposes.

'Belief systems' or 'religions'?

The use of the term 'belief systems' rather than 'religions' ensures that reference is made to other views of life which do not necessarily include a theistic or transcendent perspective. The Theravada school of Buddhism and some strands of Hinduism are of this kind. Likewise certain secular humanist philosophies, whilst not to be defined as religions, certainly embody coherent systems of belief, identifiable practices and recognisable codes of conduct.

The six major religions in Britain

For the purposes of this manual most of the examples used are drawn from the great religious traditions of the world. Reference is

BUDDHISM

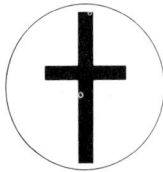

CHRISTIANITY

JUDAISM

HINDUISM

ISLAM

SIKHISM

usually made to six major religions or traditional belief systems as providing the best illustrations and examples for RE. Of course there can be no hard and fast rule here. Selection of which religions to study depends so much on varying contexts and on which criteria are used. There could, for example, be good reasons for including study of the Baha'i faith, as is now the case in some GCSE syllabuses.

However, regardless of these issues, it is evident that there is a very great difficulty in trying to give a description of each of these religions. Volumes have been written about them. Where does one begin to answer a question like 'What is Christianity?' or 'What is Hinduism?' – especially bearing in mind that we are concerned with children in a classroom? It will not do to take the answer of any one individual adherent, since that person's perspective is likely to be limited and reflect the views of a particular group. Nor is a theological or philosophical perspective much use. To distil Radhakrishnan's *Ten Principal Upanishads* or Barth's *Church Dogmatics*, even down to their most basic essentials, will not help anyone to comprehend in a complete and sufficient way the variety implied in 'Hinduism' and 'Christianity'.

There are other perspectives which have provided a more analytical approach to understanding particular belief systems. A traditional approach has been to use the perspective of history, but this can appear both arid and irrelevant unless one has some prior understanding of the living reality of the system today. A more contemporary approach is provided by the so-called 'six dimensions of religion'. This, however, still remains essentially an analytical, rather than a pedagogical, model.

In seeking to answer questions such as 'What is Christianity?' and 'What is Hinduism?' we have to make use of a more practical perspective, and one which at the same time accords with the way in which a child may begin to understand a particular tradition. In other words, it is necessary to provide a model which will make some sense of the tradition, in much the same way as other subjects in the school curriculum provide models for exploring other aspects of life.

Exploring a traditional belief system

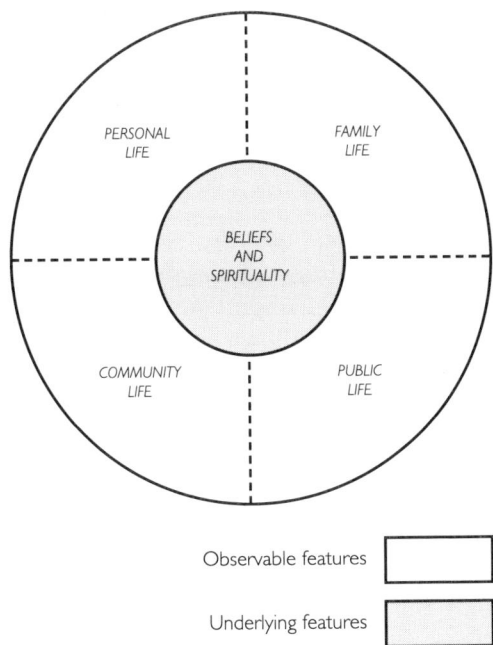

```
          PERSONAL            FAMILY
           LIFE                LIFE

                   BELIEFS
                     AND
                 SPIRITUALITY

          COMMUNITY           PUBLIC
            LIFE               LIFE
```

Observable features ▢

Underlying features ▨

Figure 3 Features of a traditional belief system

In RE children are encouraged to explore belief systems as they are encountered and expressed in the world around them. In this sense the content of their RE lessons has a practical and contemporary orientation. What children see and hear of religion in the community or on television, and what religious people do or say, are all areas of study. Observing these external features of religion is, however, only one part of making sense of a traditional belief system.

Behind all the *observable features* can be found an inner core of beliefs, values and attitudes which are hidden and cannot be observed. This inner core of *underlying features* is also an important aspect for study. The above diagram and explanation provides the model for exploring a traditional belief system in RE.

Observable features

Adherents of religious traditions engage in a wide range of activities which they associate with their particular faith. At first sight, all this activity may appear confusing. People celebrate festivals, bury their dead, meet in special places, say prayers, sing, march in public demonstrations, eat special foods, meditate and do a thousand and one other things. None of these activities in itself may be particularly unusual. What will be distinctive about them is the way in which they are performed, the context where they take place, and the meaning that is given to them. In observing these activities, therefore, it is important to look for particular aspects in order to develop an understanding of their meaning and significance. The following three are particularly important.

Symbol

Observe carefully the way in which particular places are used, the way in which they are set apart, designed and furnished for particular occasions. Notice the artefacts that are used, the way in which drama and movement may express meaning, the way in which art or music may help to convey atmosphere. All these elements invite deeper exploration of the meaning and importance that may be attached to them. The liturgy of the Orthodox churches is rich in symbol, art and drama and breathes an atmosphere of reverence, awe and wonder.

Story

Many activities (though not all, by any means) are associated with a particular story or tradition. This is often an important aspect in linking the activity with the wider concerns or traditions of the religion. At the festival of Wesak, celebrating the birth, enlightenment and death of the Buddha, it is customary for stories from the life of Siddhartha Gautama to be retold.

People

Observe those who are participating in the activities, and especially the role they play. Some will be in positions of leadership and will be the focus of attention; others will be assisting or simply participating. At a traditional Hindu funeral, we may observe the role played by the eldest son, indicating the family basis of the ritual, as well as the presence of priests and other officiants who represent the wider tradition of belief and practice.

The reason why these aspects are particularly important is that they point beyond themselves to the special meaning and significance that is attached to them. At the same time they provide a 'way in' to an exploration of religious traditions, and one that is particularly suitable at primary level.

In making these observations, we need also to be careful to explore the contexts in which the activities take place. Our diagram reminds us of the four contexts through which an exploration of a traditional belief system can be made.

Personal life

Religious behaviour is sometimes expressed in a very personal way. It is important to observe the way in which people act and express themselves as individuals. These activities may be rather different from other actions which are performed in the company of others. Individual prayer or meditation in most traditions expresses the most obvious form of religious practice of individuals.

Family life

Some religious activities are performed in the context of the family group and may be located in the home. In this case it is the actions of the family as a whole which we are observing. In a Jewish family, the observance of dietary rules is normally considered to be particularly important and the family context of many festivals and observances is seen as a key factor in maintaining and handing on Jewish traditions.

Community life

This is the likely context of many of the most significant activities of a religious tradition. Many (but certainly not all) religions express their ideas in activities which take place when the community of the faithful gather together. Although a Muslim may pray anywhere, either alone or in the family context, the gathering of Muslims for Jum'a prayers in the mosque on Fridays holds a special place in the life of the community.

Public life

All religious traditions impinge in some way on wider aspects of society. Here it is important to observe the ways in which religious communities address themselves to issues in society and proclaim and uphold their beliefs in public. We are certainly familiar with the many groups who, in the name of their religion, wish to influence society in relation to issues such as the environment, racial justice or the fair distribution of wealth.

In exploring these observable aspects and contexts, it is also important to try to explore something of the feelings and experience of the participants. Emotions of joy and solemnity, awe and wonder, calm and excitement, serenity and sadness are often to be seen in those who are caught up in giving expression to their religion.

The exploration with which we are concerned in RE, however, does not end at a mere observation of external features. These features are a means to an end. Since children will generally encounter religions in the first place by observing these external features, they have their place. But the purpose of the exercise is essentially to explore the meaning that is given to the activities. With this in mind we now turn to the inner part of the circle in our diagram to identify those features of a traditional belief system which are not easily observable.

Underlying features

At the heart of traditional belief systems, behind all their external features, can be found the inner core of faith, values and attitudes. Two main aspects of this inner core are particularly relevant for the purposes of RE – beliefs and spirituality.

Beliefs

These, of course, may be stated at different levels. Many of the beliefs to which people give expression are derived from or subsidiary to other beliefs. In this area, we are drawing attention to those beliefs which are essential to a particular tradition. In spite of differences of interpretation, they are shared by most adherents.

Christian belief in Jesus Christ as the Son of God is a belief of this kind. It is a fundamental belief, shared by all Christians, though there are varieties of interpretation among Christians as to what precisely the belief means, and there are many divisions of opinion as to what should be the appropriate way of expressing or responding to it.

The beliefs in question may not be precisely defined in any way as, for example, in a creed. They may be a general set of ideas on the basis of which groups of adherents express varying views and interpretations. The way in which they are expressed will reflect different emphases. Their importance in relation to other beliefs may vary. There is therefore no attempt to organise beliefs in any kind of hierarchy. The important thing is that they are all linked together, and, taken together, they express a distinctive world-view.

In some traditions, the absence of any credal formulation is important since the essence of that tradition is not represented by adherance to propositions of belief stated verbally, but by embracing a whole way of life and social struc-ture. Nevertheless, it is still true to say that underlying that way of life there will be certain ideas which give it shape and meaning and which are important to its identity. We have to speak in this much more tentative way when we use the word 'beliefs' in connection with the Hindu tradition. Hinduism does not have the kind of preoccupation with propositional belief which is found in some Western traditions. It would still be true to say that ideas like karma and samsara are very influential and pervasive, however ill-defined they may appear.

Spirituality

Spirituality may be described in many ways. It is difficult to offer one short definition which encompasses all the diverse understandings and beliefs about spiritual life and activity. Therefore this term is used in a broad sense to include other aspects of the inner life of human beings which may or may not be restricted to religious life and activity.

Spirituality may refer to the fact that human beings, in ways that are significantly different from other living creatures, are able to formulate and pursue a variety of ambitions, hopes and visions in relation to personal and collective achievements, lifestyles and character. Spiritual characteristics are, therefore, not the preserve of any one group of people. They are typical of human beings simply by virtue of their common human bond.

The particular spiritual characteristics which individuals acquire and exhibit emerge from complex processes which include both inherited and environmental factors. These processes also include each individual's own unique experience and his or her personal reflections on that experience. For significant numbers of people, these include experiences which are believed to be encounters with God or other transcendent realities. Experiences of this kind may or may not occur within the structures of traditional religious systems. For other people, the development of their spiritual capacities takes place with little or no experience of or belief in the supernatural. Thus spirituality, while central to religion, is not restricted to religious life and activity.

Individual spiritual characteristics arise out of the human capacity for inner development. This manifests itself in a number of ways:

1 *Transcending the immediate and the mundane.* A capacity to transcend the immediacy of natural and necessary functioning on the physical and material level is a characteristic of human nature. Indeed, many people believe that the development of this capacity is one of the distinctive indicators of what it means to be truly or fully human. It is this capacity which is stimulated by varying degrees of personal energy and inspiration to generate impressive achievements in creative imagin-ation, technological inventiveness, physical endeavours and qualities of personal character. The source of this capacity and of the energy and inspiration needed to transcend the immediate and mundane is often believed to be in God or other forms of ultimate reality. The belief that evil forces or spirits can exert a detrimental influence on the development and expression of this capacity is also part of many people's pattern of belief.

2 *Developing particular temperaments or dispositions.*
All people exhibit some predominant
temperaments or dispositions which are
central to their personalities. The patterns of
temperaments and dispositions in any individual's life often reflect some tension between
opposites such as optimism and pessimism;
contentment and dissatisfaction; cynicism and
faith. The ways in which these temperaments
and dispositions are controlled and managed
may also be seen as a significant aspect of an
individual's spirituality.

Most of the major belief systems of the world
have sets of beliefs about the origin and value
of such human capacities. They may also have
teachings and practices designed to promote
the appropriate management of these in the
lives of believers and adherents.

3 *Developing particular sets of character traits and
values.* Human beings have a capacity to
develop a set of character traits, values and
attitudes. The particular traits, values and
attitudes which individuals exhibit will be
loosely related to and reflect their predominant dispositions and temperaments. The
significant differences lie in the degree to
which such temperaments and dispositions
become firmly controlled by and consistently
expressed in the value system and lifestyle of
any individual. This very personal quality of
character may also be seen as a feature of
spirituality.

People who may have achieved a relatively
high degree of success in integrating the
diverse features of their lives into a clear sense
of personal identity and self-acceptance are
often judged as being of strong character or
spirit. This integration or wholeness may be
built around an overall sense of purpose or
meaning. It may involve a commitment to
some ideal, principle or cause. It may arise out
of habitual attempts to live by such core
human values as love, kindness, humility,
truthfulness, justice, honesty, mercy and
hospitality. It may also be centred on what is
believed to be a personal relationship with the
Divine.

It is important to note that most of the major
traditional belief systems of the world focus
on particular understandings of appropriate
character traits and values. Many of their
beliefs, teachings and practices are designed to
promote these in the lives of believers and
adherents.

4 *Awareness of being an enduring entity which
persists over time and retains a continuity of self-
consciousness and personal identity.* Most people
gradually develop an awareness of being an
enduring entity which persists over time and
retains a continuity of self-consciousness and
personal identity. This enduring, continuous
self-awareness enables individuals and groups
to look back in memory, anticipate and plan
for the future and develop consistent ideas
about themselves, others and the world. It also
enables humans to reflect on the fact and the
significance of their own birth, life and
eventual death.

A consciousness of continuity also underlines
the widely-held belief or value that who
people are, in this enduring sense, is as
important as what they know and what they
can do. It is this feature of human spirituality
which is strengthened and nurtured by
traditional beliefs in the eternal significance, if
not the survival, of each individual self, soul
or spirit.

5 *Detecting and responding to some of the wonder,
mystery and awesomeness of the natural world,
social living and personal experience.* Most people
at one time or another experience something
of the wonder, mystery and awesomeness of
life and this can be referred to as one of the
experiential aspects of human spirituality.
Many people, for example, whether they have
formal links with a religious tradition or not,
believe that they have been surrounded by a
presence or a power which is beyond themselves and perhaps of a supernatural kind.
These feelings may be evoked by a wide range
of experience and may occur in the most
unlikely ways and places. Examples of these
experiences may include a sense of calming
during an otherwise traumatic experience, an
awareness of being led in a direction not
previously considered, a sense of companion-

14

ship or even exhilaration in times of loneliness.

Apparently inexplicable happenings may also be interpreted in what many people call spiritual ways. For example, some people attribute some mysterious events to a spiritual or supernatural force intervening in and changing what would appear to be the natural or reasonably-to-be-expected outcome of a certain chain of events.

Some people are deeply moved by a seemingly fortuitous event which changes their whole life and they attribute this to the work of some spiritual force or reality. Visions and the receiving of important revelations are also found among accounts of this kind of spiritual experience. On other occasions, people claim to be healed by the direct intervention of God, often in the face of declared hopelessness. All of the religious traditions of the world are rich with accounts of these kinds of experiences of mystery, and they help to define their particular understanding of spirituality.

6 *Recognising, remembering and reliving a select number of significant experiences.* Many people point to some key experiences in the past as playing significant roles in the shaping of their individual and collective lives. Many of these experiences are so significant that they are recalled and re-experienced in various rituals and celebrations. It is from these experiences and their regular recall that the people involved draw inspiration and derive authoritative insights into the meaning and purpose of life. Participation in these rituals and celebrations is seen by many people as a deeply spiritual experience that has the potential to give specific shape to their spirituality.

All of these traditional belief systems, especially religious ones, point to certain historical, legendary or mythical events and/or charismatic people who have played key or formative roles in shaping the tradition. These events and people are also believed to be the expressions, par excellence, of spiritual life and experience. In some traditions, rituals and ceremonies are expressly designed to perpetuate these events and people as living realities in the modern community of believers. Participation in these rituals is an essential part of the spirituality of those who share the tradition.

For example, in the Christian tradition, Jesus shares in a last meal with his disciples just before death, and this is a key formative experience in the shaping of the tradition. For many Christians sharing in the sacramental rituals which recall this experience provides a significant means of spiritual growth. In the Muslim tradition, during the fast of Ramadan, believers recall the unique moment of revelation of the Qur'an on the Night of Power, and as it were, relive the experience. For Jewish people, the annual festival of Passover recalls the exodus from slavery in Egypt in ancient times. All of the contemporary rituals, especially those related to the Seder meal, are designed to recall the events and stories and to play a highly formative role in perpetuating Jewish identity.

When dealing with this aspect of the underlying qualities of traditions, it is important that at least these understandings of the concept of spirituality are dealt with. As a general rule of thumb, they are better studied through biographical material in the primary school and in a more abstract way in the secondary school.

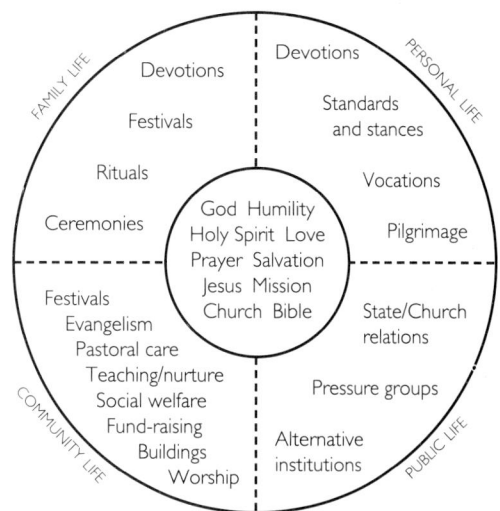

Figure 4 Features of Christianity

15

Figures 4 and 5 illustrate examples of these inter-relationships from the Christian and Jewish traditions.

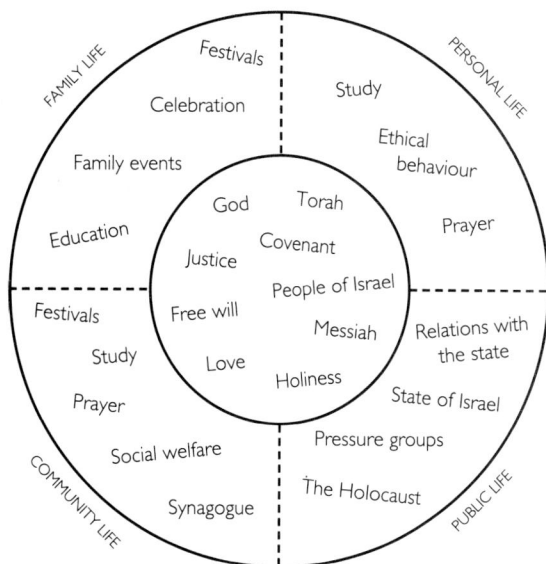

Figure 5 Features of Judaism

Traditional belief systems: classroom guidelines

The model we have used is intended essentially to help teachers to identify the kind of material that can be used in the classroom and to give them an overview of how religious traditions might be viewed in an educational context. Here are four guidelines to be followed when exploring traditional belief systems in RE:

1 Identify suitable topics.
2 Be aware of different perspectives within traditions.
3 Aim for an objective, fair and balanced presentation.
4 Ensure that a variety of different traditional belief systems are explored.

Suitable topics

When it comes to the question of identifying topics for RE from the major religious traditions,

it is important that teachers pay careful regard to those areas and emphases that the tradition itself would identify as significant. Within each tradition there are a number of these key topics, but there is not usually a common theme which would link them together across all the traditions. For example, in Islam the Hajj would be such a key topic. On the other hand, the theme of 'pilgrimage' would not feature as such a major topic in the exploration of Christianity.

In any RE programme including an exploration of Christianity we would expect to find units of work dealing with such things as baptism, Holy Communion, the Bible, Easter, the Church. These are examples of the kind of topics which would be of importance to nearly all Christians, even though there will be a wide variety of expression and interpretation in relation to them. Key topics are found in all traditions. Teachers should consult the teacher's manuals, *Christianity, Islam,* and *Judaism,* where examples of these topics are given in more detail. The model we have been using provides a focus for teachers to consider some of the aspects and contexts through which the selected topics can be explored in the classroom – at a level suitable for the age range of the children. Within particular traditions, the topics themselves will determine some of these factors. In many cases, however, it will be possible to choose from a number of different contexts and aspects. The topic of Christian baptism, for example, could be explored in a personal, family or religious community context. The different aspects of the topic could be selected according to the teacher's objectives and the age of the children.

Different perspectives

A second major question is concerned with the perspective through which each tradition is approached. We have indicated that it cannot be the perspective of any one believer. That perspective might convey some real understanding of what it means to be committed to a religion and way of life, but it is unlikely to be representative of the tradition as a whole. It will tend to regard as secondary – even to denigrate or disparage – the perspective of some other believers. While it is essential in RE that children are able to listen to, observe and explore the faith of believers, they should not limit themselves to one single perspective. They should recognise from an early stage that people differ in their perspectives. They should be encouraged to take a broad view of a tradition as a whole; that will mean, in theory at least, that the faith and outlook of anyone who claims to belong to a tradition may be explored by the children.

Objective presentation

If we are to help children observe a tradition as a whole, it follows that the presentation we give will aim to be as objective, fair and balanced as possible. This means that due weight will need to be given to different emphases, and teachers will need to take into consideration how they achieve a balance between some of the contrasting elements set out below.

The essential and the cultural

Some of the observable features which may be explored in the classroom will be common to all those who share a tradition. The celebration of Passover within Judaism is a common essential feature. On the other hand, the way in which it is celebrated will vary, sometimes according to Sephardi or Ashkenazi traditions, and sometimes according to national traditions. The celebration of Christmas is broadly universal within the Christian Church, but many of its elements (e.g. the mid-winter setting) are culturally determined in the northern hemisphere; other elements (e.g. the place given to St Nicholas in the celebrations) vary according to national boundaries.

The majority and the minority

In presenting any tradition, it is clearly important that children are made aware of the way in which the majority express their faith and commitment. At the same time, since they need to appreciate different expressions and viewpoints, due regard will need to be given to some of those aspects and emphases which are represented by minorities. For example, since within the Christian tradition as a whole the Roman Catholic Church represents the majority of Christians, some knowledge and appreciation of Roman Catholicism and its emphases is basic to an understanding of the tradition as a whole. The Quakers, on the other hand, are a very small group and so constitute a minority within the large family of Christian traditions. Nevertheless, an understanding of their tradition is also important since it provides a contrast of interpretation and practice. We could say the same about the Sufi tradition in Islam, or the Hasidim in Judaism.

The local and the global

The basis for the exploration of a religious tradition will, in many cases, be found within a local community. Where possible, it is highly desirable that children should have first-hand access to a living and local expression of faith. This should not, however, form their total perspective, since it could as a result be distorted in a number of ways. This applies particularly to those religious groups which have settled in the United Kingdom relatively recently, and who have been acutely aware of the need both to preserve their distinctiveness and to conform with local dictates. For example, the way in which Sikh and Hindu groups tend to meet regularly and congregationally on Sunday is dictated by local conditions and would not be representative of Sikhism or Hinduism in India. Moreover, the way in which particular groups practise their faith may not be wholly typical. For example, the celebrations of Diwali in the United Kingdom are drawn mainly from northern Indian traditions, and are less typical of southern Indians, who are in a small minority in Britain.

The popular and the intellectual

A tension has always existed between the great mass of practitioners and those teachers and exponents who have absorbed their tradition at the philosophical level. Popular forms of art, music or devotion may appear crude and unsophisticated to a guru or theologian. At the same time, many practitioners of religions see the concerns of the intellectuals, or philosophers within their tradition as largely irrelevant to the way religion is lived and practised. This dichotomy is well illustrated in the way different groups describe or conceptualise God, ranging from very mundane and concrete images to highly abstract concepts. At a practical level it may be observed in the different attitudes found within the Hindu tradition, in which the deities represented in popular images are regarded by other Hindus as useful but inessential aids to the practice of devotion. We may observe the same tendency in traditions which place much greater emphasis on the verbal expression of religion, some insisting on the literal truth of what is written, and others insisting on the need to interpret verbal images. In RE it is important that children explore the popular dimension since it is the one which they are initially most likely to encounter. At the same time, they should gradually appreciate more symbolic expressions of the same tradition.

The traditional and the radical

These two are closely related to the popular and intellectual interpretations, but are not identical to them. They are found especially in relation to two areas. In the first instance, in the area of worship and rituals, traditionalists seek to maintain the form of a tradition in contrast to the radicals who seek to keep alive the spirit of a tradition – in some cases with little regard for the traditional form. The second is the ethical area, where traditionalists will tend to hold on to a literal interpretation of traditional codes and to apply them literally to contemporary situations; radicals, on the other hand, tend to apply traditional codes to contemporary situations by seeking to interpret the spirit of the code in the light of new considerations and changing circumstances. Significant examples of this contrast are most apparent when considering some contemporary moral issues. At a later stage in their schooling children should be developing an awareness of the different approaches to issues represented by these contrasting attitudes. A similar pattern is found in the contrast between those who view their own tradition as uniquely authentic and adopt an exclusive attitude to those who do not share it and those, on the other hand, who see their own tradition in a way that permits them to adopt a more inclusive attitude to those who do not share the same beliefs and traditions.

Exploring a variety of traditional belief systems

This leads to the last question, that of achieving an overall balance in exploring religious traditions within a 5–16 RE programme. As we noted on page 1, the 1988 Education Reform Act states quite clearly that RE should include the study of Christianity and 'the other principal religious traditions in Great Britain'. The six major religious traditions will certainly feature in the total programme, but it is not necessary for the purpose of a balanced RE programme that children should explore all six in equal measure.

Certainly by the end of schooling pupils should have at least a basic knowledge of the six major religious traditions. It is important, however, that they avoid the confusion that comes from a superficial fact-gathering exercise. The following principles are important when seeking a balanced RE programme 5–16. By the age of sixteen pupils should have:

- developed a basic understanding of and be able to recognise the main features of the six traditions;
- considered non-religious ideas and ideals;
- had the opportunity, as far as possible, to explore their own particular tradition in an educational context;
- developed a deeper understanding of at least two and no more than three of the six traditions: one of these should be the Christian tradition.

This final guideline does not deny the importance of approaching all religions on the same educational basis which gives parity of esteem to each. However, the balance of religions to be studied is a matter for local authorities to decide.

Shared human experience

What is meant by 'shared human experience'? In the first place, we are concerned with experiences which are widely shared. We are not looking at the unique experiences of millions of isolated individuals but at the kind of experiences which fall to most human beings. Secondly, we are looking at experiences which are not the preserve of any one group of people, but at those which are typical of human beings simply by virtue of their common human bond. In the third place we are concerned with particularly significant experiences. For our purposes, the experiences which are regarded as significant are those which have prompted, and continue to prompt, the puzzling or ultimate questions about life.

It is difficult to portray such a fluid thing as human experience as a model but Figure 6 given below emphasises the process of involving children in exploring their own and other people's experiences of life in order that they may begin to raise and consider the important issues and ultimate questions that underlie and arise out of our shared human experience.

Therefore an exploration of human experience is again an exploration of observable and underlying features. It is the latter which give significance to the former. It may, therefore, be more useful in this case to begin by referring to these underlying features.

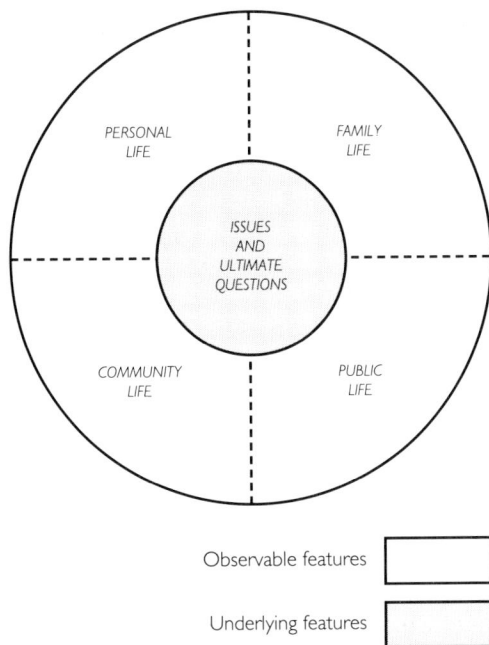

Observable features

Underlying features

Figure 6 Features of shared human experience

Underlying features

Ultimate questions

It is by no means easy to give a clear definition of ultimate questions. They are sometimes referred to as unanswerable questions – but are these questions unanswerable because of our lack of sufficient knowledge, or because, as some assert, they are meaningless? Moreover, although there is a sense in which they are unanswerable, it is curious how human beings are forever answering them. They are not, of course, answering them with verifiable statements of fact. People usually preface their answers with such words as 'I/we believe ...' for these questions can only be answered by an expression of belief, a statement of faith.

Whether the questions appear to be meaningless or not, they are certainly those which have engaged the sharpest minds and stirred the deepest emotions. The answers that are given are fundamental to all outlooks on life, non-religious or religious. Not everyone, by any means, asks these questions all the time, or in the same form, or with the same force or urgency; yet they have a habit of recurring and seem inescapable. They are ultimate questions in the sense that they ask about ultimate things – questions beyond which there are no more questions; questions 'at the end of the line'.

It may be helpful if we identify these questions as being concerned with a number of general areas of human experience, as represented in Figure 7. All these general areas are interrelated with the ultimate question 'What does it mean to be human?' The answer we give to that question will normally define and shape the answers we give to the other questions – or vice versa. Those who believe that human beings are the end product of a long chain of random selection, or the byproducts of an ongoing historical process, or eternal and immaterial souls confined in a temporal and material body, or the children of a loving and compassionate God, will all have widely differing perspectives when it comes to looking at the other questions.

Each of these general areas gives rise to a number of more detailed questions, which have this

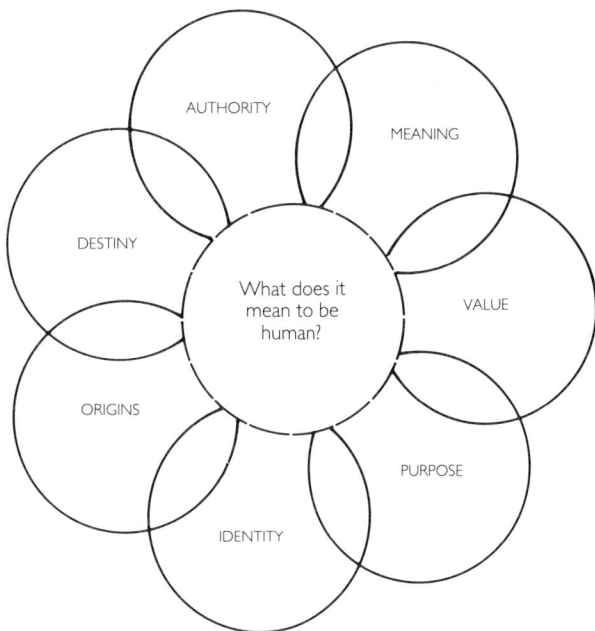

Figure 7 Areas concerned with ultimate questions

GENERAL AREA	EXAMPLE QUESTIONS
Authority	Why should I do as you say? Is there a God? Who says I shouldn't steal?
Meaning	Why do the innocent suffer? Where is happiness to be found? What is truth?
Value	What is most important to me? Do people matter more than things? Why don't we care?
Purpose	What is life for? What is success? What should my ambition be?
Identity	Who am I? Who do I belong to? Does it matter if we are different?
Origins	Why did the world begin? Where is the source of life to be found? When does life start?
Destiny	Is there life after death? What future is there for us? What will become of me?

Figure 8 Ultimate questions

ultimate dimension to them. The questions may be very general, or they may be couched in more personal terms. Those which are given in Figure 8 as examples – and there are many more – are not by any means confined to just one of the general areas we have identified. They overlap very considerably.

Issues and experiences

A wide range of issues and experiences underlie the ultimate questions, and often give rise to them. This is because the questions themselves have an important existential and emotional dimension to them. They are not merely the ramblings of abstract thinkers. The reasons why the questions are so important and so persistent is that they arise out of some of our deepest emotions and our most compelling experiences. The feelings and experiences are closely interwoven, and we are unwise to try to distinguish too sharply between them.

The kinds of experiences to which we refer are those which often come to the surface in crisis situations – when people are confronted with difficult decisions, or faced with impossible circumstances, or overwhelmed by insoluble problems. The pain of suffering ('Why should

this happen to me?') or the approach of death ('Is there any future?'); deciding about the future, whether one's own or another's ('Should I have an abortion?'); or trying to find solutions to seemingly intractable problems of personal and social relationships ('Should I get married?', 'How should we combat racism?'); these are all pressing situations which force upon us questions of purpose or meaning, authority or identity. Feelings of fear or doubt, guilt or helplessness may amplify the problem and make a solution even more pressing.

There are other experiences which come to people in unexpected ways – experiences which heighten the emotions and sometimes open up questions not usually considered before. Experiences of awe, wonder, mystery or beauty are of this kind. They may come to people when they suddenly become aware of the powerful forces of nature or when they hold a newborn child, and they may inspire feelings of fear, joy or devotion.

There are feelings, too, which derive from an ongoing awareness of human finiteness and the uncertainty of life, or from a sense of responsibility for the world we live in and those around us. At the same time, we should not confine ourselves just to those feelings and experiences which appear to be problematic, or serious, or negative or morbid. Many of the important questions of life come to light through experiences of great joyfulness, celebration and ecstasy; and human beings have a great capacity for responding in positive ways to the difficulties and hardships of life.

It is not surprising, therefore, that the kind of feelings we are concerned with here are found in pairs of opposites – joy and sorrow, certainty and doubt, belonging and loneliness, hope and despair, love and hate. They represent the great range of emotions through which people express themselves, and through which they respond both to the unexpected and the inevitable.

Observable features

Ultimate questions and underlying feelings and responses are, however, intangible. They only become evident through the observable behaviour that people use to express themselves in particular situations. Figure 6 on page 19 focuses on four contexts in which this observable behaviour can be explored. All four contexts – personal life, family life, community life and public life – are important in order that a balanced approach may be achieved. Once again an excessive concentration on individual behaviour, for example, may fail to raise issues quite as sharply as they could be raised by exploring situations in other contexts.

When we were dealing with traditional belief systems, we found that examples of observable behaviour could be identified and described with relative ease – celebrating festivals, performing rituals, meeting in buildings and so on. With the use of suitable resources these can all be brought into the classroom for children to explore.

This exercise is less easy with regard to shared human experience where any human behaviour or situation could be used as a basis for exploration, and where, on the whole, it is impossible to specify in advance the particular behaviours and situations which might serve as illustrations. Of course, specific religious activities can (and should) themselves be used as illustrations, since they are part of human experience.

In RE, the guiding principle in identifying an appropriate behaviour or situation must always be that it has the greatest potential for raising ultimate questions and for exploring the issues and experiences that underlie them.

Shared human experience: classroom guidelines

While it is not so easy to identify quickly the kind of themes or situations which best serve this exploration of shared human experience, it is possible to suggest the sort of categories or themes which offer a potential wealth of suitable material.

The general categories identified in Figure 9 provide an indication of the sorts of specific themes from which classroom topics may be chosen. Teachers will be aware of other suitable categories and will be able to draw on their own knowledge and experiences in choosing the best examples.

When identifying suitable classroom topics it is useful to recognise that:

- many of the shared human experience topics are likely to be explored from different perspectives in other areas of the curriculum. Careful liaison between teachers and departments is essential;
- the distinctive perspective of RE should be carefully preserved when a topic crosses subject boundaries;
- the essential value of dealing with shared human experience topics in RE lies in their potential for raising ultimate questions and exploring a variety of possible answers;
- an appropriate way of dealing with shared human experience in RE is to use the life themes approach. Information about this can be found on page 41–2.

CATEGORIES OF HUMAN EXPERIENCE	POTENTIAL AREAS FOR IDENTIFYING TOPICS
The natural world	Human awareness of the world about us – the orderliness of nature, regularity of seasons, resources for food, energy and wealth; the awe-inspiring aspects, natural wonders and disasters, power of natural forces; the interrelatedness of all living things; the vastness of the universe and the details of the microcosm; the origins and future of the earth; the natural life cycle.
Relationships	Relationships of friendship and enmity, both personal and social; the family and relationships within the family; belonging to groups based on interest, cause or belief; relationships of equality, superiority or inferiority; personal, familial, social and national identity.
Rules and issues	The rules by which people live; codes of behaviour; legal and moral rules; personal and social moral issues, such as war and peace, inequality, human rights, poverty and affluence, law and order, euthanasia and abortion, the environment, democracy.
Stages of life	The human life process and the changes in outlook that growth and decay bring; experiences associated with childbirth, maturation, old age and death; rites of passage, particularly those associated with birth, initiation, marriage and death.
Celebrations	Ceremonies which mark important occasions in personal and community life; birthdays, anniversaries, festivals, fasts and solemn days; community, national and religious occasions; celebrations of events, people and values.
Lifestyles	The way of living that people adopt as an expression of their identity, belief or culture; customs of food and clothing; communal, regimented and independent lifestyles, monastic and ascetic patterns of living; competitive and cooperative lifestyles, lifestyles which represent a non-conformist reaction to current norms, e.g. vegetarianism.
Suffering	Human suffering as a result of disease, natural disasters, accidents; suffering as a result of war, violence and other conflict; cruelty to other human beings and animals; persecution, racial discrimination, and oppression in any form; the Holocaust; human responses to the problems of evil and suffering.

Figure 9 Categories and areas for exploring shared human experience

Individual patterns of belief

It may appear strange to single out patterns of belief of individuals as a potential area to be included in RE. This does not, however, refer to individuals in a general sense, but to those individuals, both teachers and pupils, in a particular class at a particular time. It is essential to remember in RE that potential content is located not only outside the classroom, but is also present in the classroom.

There are at least three good reasons why this area is important, and why it is to be distinguished from the others.

1 It is inevitable that both children and teachers will bring into the classroom their own personal beliefs, sense of identity, attitudes and experiences. In the case of the children,

their experiences may be few and their beliefs, attitudes and sense of identity may be embryonic, but they are of great importance because these are the materials of the subject of RE which are closest and most accessible to the children and are therefore of most relevance to them. They include those experiences which are most immediate to them, as well as those which apparently assume the greatest importance for them. Because of this relevance and immediacy for individuals, particular experiences, perceptions and behaviour may be held to be not only significant, but also normative – the way I perceive things is the way everyone perceives things. That, of course, is not true, but for the purposes of RE, it is a distinctive and important perception. RE is concerned to develop and broaden that perspective. It is, however, very important to respect 'where children are'. In seeking to develop and broaden an individual's perspective, the teacher of RE must be very careful not to undermine those aspects of a person's life which have played a large part in his or her development.

2 It is evident that the beliefs and behaviour that children bring into the classroom will have been informed and influenced by a whole range of factors. How far these influences impinge on children will vary from individual to individual. Some may have a very strong sense of identity, derived from their own family or cultural group. Others may not. The point is, however, that it is highly unlikely that any individual will conform entirely with externally imposed norms. A number of other factors will have influenced their perception. While they may conform outwardly, in many cases they do, in fact, see things quite differently. They may use the language handed on to them by others, but their actual understanding of what it means may be far from what is intended. It is equally true as a general principle that individual patterns of belief and behaviour rarely conform in detail with group norms.

3 Education – and, more specifically, RE – is not primarily concerned with children as recipients of information, suitably packaged and delivered to them, or as units to be trained or indoctrinated in cultural norms. If it were, then the perceptions and sense of identity of individuals could have no real relevance as potential content. They only assume major significance where the educational goals are directed specifically to the child's own beliefs and values and are encouraging constructive and creative thinking about these beliefs and values.

Exploring individual patterns of belief

For the purpose of clarifying this third area of potential content for RE, the same basic design for a diagram taken from the RE field of enquiry applies.

It is not necessary in this case to break down each of the parts of this diagram in detail. The observable features of individuals may once

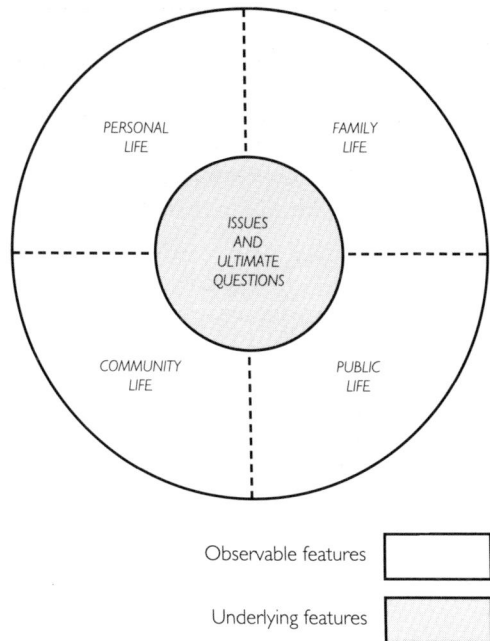

Figure 10   Features of individual patterns of belief

again be explored in the same four contexts. There is also a progression from behaviour through feelings and experiences to the child's own beliefs and values – the underlying features.

It is clearly impossible to define beforehand the pattern of behaviour, experience and value that each child will bring into the classroom. It will vary greatly from child to child, class to class, age to age. The essential point, however, is that this area is as important as the other two as a source of potential content for exploration in the class-room. Reference should be constantly made to this area in any teaching programme. Although it cannot be planned as part of the formal curriculum of the subject, it is of the greatest importance.

The way in which individual patterns of belief emerge in the classroom and become material for exploration is entirely informal and ad hoc. An objection might arise in discussion; a child may point out a quite different way of looking at something; a question may be raised at the start of the lesson such as 'Miss, Tracey and I have been arguing about what happens to you when you die. What do you think?' or 'Miss, my Dad

23

doesn't agree with that' or 'Sir, when we have Diwali, we read a different story'. The teacher of RE cannot of course plan ahead for these reactions and contributions. On the other hand, the sensitive teacher will always be looking for opportunities to include and develop these more personal and individual contributions in a way which may benefit the whole class.

Interrelationships within the field of enquiry

We have so far examined three main areas as sources of content for RE. Any programme of RE that fails to help children explore all three areas will in some way fail to achieve the aim of the subject. To concentrate on one area at the expense of the others will distort it. Yet the three areas are not chosen randomly nor are they identified as three distinct entities. They are closely related to each other, and this interrelationship is itself an essential part of the field of enquiry of the subject.

The point is emphasised in Figure 11, which indicates the way in which each area relates to and influences the others.

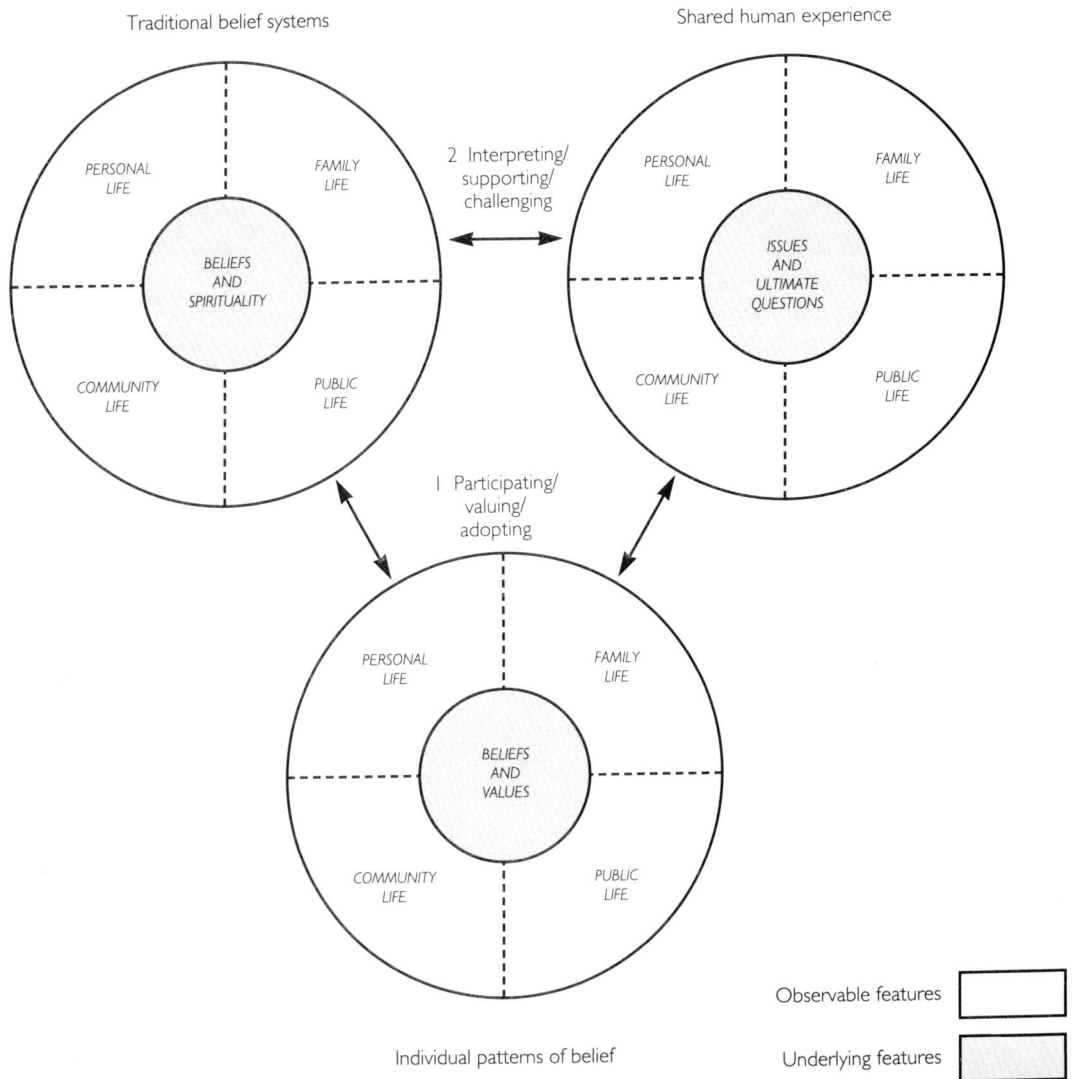

Figure 11 Interrelationships within the RE field of enquiry

Links with individual patterns of belief

The first of these relationships (marked 1 in Figure 11) is that which links individual patterns of belief – in our case those of the child and the teacher in the classroom – with shared human experience and with traditional belief systems. The arrows indicate a two-way relationship between the individual and the other two areas. This relationship can be characterised by the use of the words 'participating', 'valuing' and 'adopting'. These point to the different levels at which we all relate to the total experience, knowledge and achievements of humanity, including those enshrined in the traditional belief systems.

Participating

All people obviously participate in the general shared experience of humanity in some way or another and at one level or another. Many pupils will be aware of the big questions which life presents. They will have had experiences which highlight life's mystery and challenge, including some that suggest the possibility of transcendent realities.

Equally, all individuals participate in particular cultures. We cannot jump out of our historical and cultural skins. We are related in some way to particular traditional belief systems. They contribute to our identity and we participate in their ongoing life.

Valuing

All individuals, however, engage in a process of selection in relation to life's experiences and the traditions to which we belong. Some aspects become increasingly valuable to us and others cease to attract our attention. The pupils' maturity in relation to their own pattern of belief and behaviour is enhanced as they discover those aspects of life which are becoming more important to them and those which have little or no value to them.

Adopting

At another level many individuals consciously go beyond a simple participation in the culturally conditioned life about them. They identify with certain groups, lifestyles and value systems and adopt a particular way of life. Certain human and/or traditional characteristics are seen not only as being important and valuable, they become the focal point of the individual's own sense of identity.

In reality, relationships between individuals and systems are rarely as simple as the above analysis suggests. Yet it is clearly possible to observe these different levels of response. They may be illustrated, for example, by the way in which Christmas is celebrated in Britain today. Some people will carry on the tradition without considering its origin or religious significance. Others will attach value to what it represents in a general kind of way. Others will see it as a highlight of their own faith and commitment.

Links with shared human experience

The second relationship with which we are concerned (marked 2 in Figure 11) is that which links traditional belief systems with shared human experience. Again the double-headed arrow suggests a two-way relationship and we use three words to describe something of the essential characteristics of this complex relationship.

Interpreting

There is a very real sense in which the traditional belief systems exist to provide a framework of understanding and way of responding to the mysteries and challenges of human life. In some cases this interpreting quality may be seen as providing answers, on the basis of faith, to ultimate questions. In others it may take the form of providing a framework in which the questions remain open and mysterious.

Supporting

There is also a kind of psychological dimension to the relationship between the belief systems and human experience. The experience of being human does not simply pose questions at an intellectual level. It also presents problems at an emotional level. In particular there are experiences which shatter confidence and undermine the fabric of life, as well as those which stimulate determination and courage. At this point the various belief systems provide, in their own ways, means for supporting those who need help and encouragement and outlets for courageous and adventurous exploits.

Challenging

Thirdly, the traditional belief systems offer important challenges to what might generally be believed, valued and done by the majority of people at a given time. Because they encapsulate ideals, visions and ultimate goals, they often have the capacity to call on people to rise above their immediate circumstances and to pursue nobler ends. They can suggest new ways of looking at things, open up new horizons and possibilities and raise new questions about life. Similarly, developments within shared human experience can and often do present challenges to the traditions to re-think, or at least re-express, some of their basic beliefs and commitments.

Summary

We are now in a position to summarise the important points made in the preceding section.

1 Figure 11 on page 24 is essentially a content model in as much as it sets out the RE field of enquiry or the potential range of content that the subject may explore. However, these are not separate, static bodies of knowledge, but a dynamic whole.

The process of RE involves children in exploring this whole through a variety of approaches. This process of exploration involves a dynamic relationship between the children and the main areas of content which have been described.

2 Therefore the process involves the movement from the outside (observable) parts of the model to the inside (underlying) parts of the model. This relationship is paramount as RE is primarily about the exploration of meaning. The exploration of the observable should involve children in using all of their senses.

3 The exploration of observable phenomena can be conceptualised in four contexts: individual, family, community and public life. Teachers may then plan appropriate topics drawn from these four contexts.

How the selection of material from these contexts relates to curriculum planning appropriate to a particular Key Stage is developed in Part Three of this manual.

2 Concepts, attitudes, skills and knowledge

Teachers of RE, as teachers of other subjects, have the task of helping children to develop their understanding by encouraging them to acquire and use a range of concepts, skills, attitudes and knowledge. We use this sequence of elements in the RE programme because it represents the priorities for what we are trying to achieve in RE. Briefly this sequence consists of the following aspects:

- Identifying the concept(s) we hope to develop through a particular topic
- Considering the attitudes we hope the learning experience will promote
- Deciding if there are particular skills which children need to develop to help them assimilate the concepts and attitudes we are considering
- Selecting the appropriate knowledge or content which will best help to develop the concepts, skills and attitudes we have identified.

Concepts

Concepts are essentially ideas which help us and our children make sense of our experiences of a great variety of things, objects, information, events and occurrences.

When we were looking at the field of enquiry we drew attention in particular to the distinction between those aspects which may be observed and those which may be inferred. That there is a relationship between the two is obvious. It is in the exploration of this relationship that concepts are particularly important.

For example, if children are exploring the Christian practice of baptism, they may be helped to understand what is being done and said if they can begin to relate their observations to such concepts as initiation and ritual, and to Christian concepts of salvation and the Holy Spirit.

Concepts such as initiation and ritual are not incidental to RE. They give shape to the task in

which the subject is engaged. They provide a means by which children can begin to make links with other aspects of the field of enquiry and, in particular, links between the three main areas; traditional belief systems, shared human experience and individual patterns of belief.

In RE, we are concerned with helping children to develop concepts which relate to the exploration of ultimate questions and shared human experience. Although such concepts are not in themselves religious, they deal with areas of our experience which we may describe as spiritual. They are closely related to the concepts of religions but have a wider reference. Here we are considering such ideas as authority and meaning, freedom and devotion, relationship and community.

There is also a place in RE for helping children to develop general concepts which will enable them to deal with religious traditions. These concepts include myth, scripture, deity and interpretation. Figure 12 illustrates some examples.

ULTIMATE QUESTIONS	SHARED HUMAN EXPERIENCES	STUDY OF RELIGION
Authority	Awe/Wonder	Asceticism
Destiny	Celebration	Belief
Human Nature	Commitment	Deity
Identity	Community	Fundamentalism
Meaning	Devotion	Ideology
Origin	Evil	Initiation
Purpose	Freedom	Interpretation
Value	Goodness	Liberalism
	Justice/Fairness	Lifestyle
	Motivation	Monotheism
	Mystery	Morality
	Peace	Mysticism
	Relationship	Myth
	Spirituality	Orthodoxy
	Suffering	Religion
	Truth	Ritual
	Wholeness	Scripture
	Unity	Symbolism
		Worship

Figure 12   General concepts and their relation to spiritual experience/study of religion

Concepts within traditional belief systems

There are also concepts which belong within particular traditions and which are related closely to the key beliefs and values of these traditions, as shown in Figure 13 for example. Children need to become familiar with these concepts. For example, in learning about Christianity they will need to develop an understanding of such concepts as God the Father, Jesus the Christ, Holy Spirit, salvation, mission, etc. In studying Islam, concepts such as *tawhid*, *wahy*, *Shari'ah* and *din* would be important.

It is also important to note that any appreciation of traditional belief systems will involve children in acquiring and using a range of technical terms. These terms are essentially descriptive rather than conceptual. Words such as *gurdwara*, priest, Qur'an and *sangha* enable children to make clear identifications and to be accurate in their descriptions. There will, of course, be points where some of the technical terms used are also concepts – for example *sangha*.

Concept development

The kind of concepts we deal with in RE suggest the need to avoid the idea that children move methodically from simple to complex concepts.

The pattern is rather that children should understand the same concepts at an increasingly sophisticated level. In RE most of the concepts are such that a linear development of this sort is most unlikely. This is because the concepts themselves are not simply abstractions to be grasped from a variety of information. They contain what is usually called an affective dimension; that is, they can only be fully understood, or best understood, if the learner is willing and able to invest an element of personal reflection and awareness into understanding them.

For example, understanding a concept in RE such as freedom involves more than simply analysing what freedom means. It involves a degree of empathy and reflection about what it feels like to me to be free, about why freedom matters and about why other people value freedom so highly, including those for whom freedom has a religious dimension. In other words, freedom is a concept to be experienced and reflected on, not merely analysed, if it is to be understood in RE.

Thus the understanding of concepts is linked to the development of other abilities, such as the willingness to reflect on one's own experience, readiness to enter imaginatively into the experiences of others, the ability to use language and other forms of expression creatively to express these experiences and willingness to accept the limitations of our understanding. In

BUDDHIST	CHRISTIAN	HINDU	JEWISH	MUSLIM	SIKH
Anatta	Church	Ahimsa	Berakhah	Akhirah	Anand
Anicca	Eternal Life	Atman	Brit	Allah	Gurmukh
Buddha	Faith	Avatar	Elohim/Adonai	Din	Guru
Dhamma	God the Father	Bhakti	Halakhah	Ibadah	Hauma
Dukkha	Holy Spirit	Brahman	Israel	Ihsan	Jivan Mukt
Kamma	Jesus the Christ	Dharma	Kashrut	Iman	Khalsa
Metta	Love	Karma	Kedusha	Islam	Sadhana
Nibbana	Mission	Maya	Mitzvah	Jihad	Sat Nam
Sangha	Mother of God	Moksha	Shalom	Risalah	Seva
Tanha	Resurrection	Samsara	Teshuvah	Shari'ah	Sikh
	Salvation	Shakti	Torah	Shirk	
	Sin	Smriti	Tzedekah	Sunnah	
	Trinity	Sruti		Tawhid	
	Word of God	Varana		Ummah	
	Unity	Yoga		Wahy	

Figure 13 A selection of concepts within six religious traditions represented in Britain

practice this means that we may well expect children to develop a more sophisticated understanding of concepts, but their understanding may actually regress as well as progress because the active involvement and personal capacity to reflect has diminished (for a whole range of possible reasons). Thus a Key Stage One (lower primary) child may have a very basic and unsophisticated notion of freedom and a highly developed sense of what it means to be free, and in Key Stage Four (upper secondary) these two levels of understanding may be reversed.

Nevertheless, in RE we do aim towards a process of development that provides stimulus for progress both in the cognitive and affective dimensions of concepts. Thus we hope that children in all Key Stages will develop their understanding of the same concepts, but in an increasingly sophisticated way. On the one level, the expansion of their knowledge should mean that their understanding is based on a wider framework of information. On the other level, the broadening of their experience and their capacity to reflect should mean that their understanding is also based on deeper personal insight and awareness of others. This is rather different from the process of concept development in science, for example:

> Conceptual understanding of Earth science ideas develops through the key stages. Using the concept of the mineral as an example, the starting point is that young children are able to sort solids using simple criteria such as colour and feel. From here they progress to viewing a mineral as a naturally occurring solid with a set of properties (shape, hardness, colour, etc). In Key Stage Three they build on this by seeing these properties of minerals as quantifiable, for example hardness, density and composition. A full, chemical appreciation follows when they conceptualise a mineral as a naturally occurring chemical element or compound with a definite crystalline structure.

> *Non-Statutory Guidance for Science*, NCC, 1989

Attitudes

It is important to make the point that RE does not distinguish itself from the rest of the curriculum simply on the grounds that it is the RE teacher's

responsibility to promote certain attitudes. The idea that children should learn to respect each other, be polite to each other, show care and concern for others and be enthusiastic about their work is applicable throughout the curriculum and to all activities with the school. RE, of course, contributes to the encouragement of positive attitudes in these matters, but so do PE, Art, Science and the way the playground is supervised.

There are other, more specific attitudes that have to do with the educational enterprise in school which all teachers also wish to see encouraged and developed. These include such matters as developing a sense of curiosity or developing sensitivity to the living and non-living environment. Both of these are mentioned in non-statutory guidance for Science, but they are equally applicable to RE or Art or Geography.

However, other attitudes are also fundamental to the development of RE. They are not exclusive to RE, but they do arise from the nature of the subject matter with which RE deals and from the processes involved in teaching RE. For example, a willingness to value diversity in religion, culture and ethnic origin is basic to any discourse or interaction in the RE classroom. It is an attitude which a sensitive teacher will wish to see developed in all children in the classroom from the beginning of their schooling. The same would apply to helping children develop a sense of mystery, awe and wonder at the world about them. Figure 14 illustrates some of the kinds of attitudes which RE seeks to promote.

Skills

In recent years the area of skills in relation to curriculum planning has been very controversial. The controversy in History between proponents of a skills-based curriculum and proponents of a knowledge-based curriculum is one such example.

Indeed there is some dispute as to what is meant by skills and whether all skills are of the same nature. For example, does the skill of threading a needle belong to the same category as a skill involved in the process of reading? Furthermore,

GENERAL EDUCATIONAL ATTITUDES	ATTITUDES EMPHASISED IN RE
Children should be encouraged to develop the following: • a sense of curiosity • respect for evidence • a willingness to tolerate uncertainty • perseverance in applying themselves to tasks • self-confidence • sensitivity to the living and non-living environment • a sense of fairness in relationships • compassion and concern for those in need.	Children should be encouraged to develop the following: • a sense of mystery and fascination about the world • a willingness to acknowledge the needs, feelings and aspirations of others • respect for others, and willingness to learn from their insights • respect for the freedom to practise or not to practise religion • a willingness to recognise that beliefs and ideas may be expressed in a variety of ways • willingness to acknowledge the controversial and ambiguous nature of many issues about beliefs and values • confidence in their own sense of identity • willingness to value diversity in religion and culture.

Figure 14   Attitudes in RE

there is often a lack of clarity about what is meant by saying that RE should be 'skills-based'.

Our conclusion is that there are no skills peculiar to RE, and that RE does not concern itself with particular manipulative skills such as 'measuring', 'constructing', or 'making'. There is no RE equivalent to mapping skills in Geography or reading skills in English or to learning to play an instrument in Music. Nor are we *primarily* concerned in RE with the development of general educational skills such as the ability to listen attentively or to gather and record information. These form part of any educational programme and are best related to subject content.

RE should not be used simply as a vehicle for developing general educational skills, but these skills will play a part in RE as in all other curriculum areas. Finally, when we refer to skills in RE, we are not speaking about the general cognitive processes which have to do with knowing and understanding, such as classification, analysis and evaluation.

Skills emphasised in RE

The skills which are emphasised in RE are those which help children to acquire and develop the concepts and attitudes which are the focal points

of the subject. None of these skills is the sole preserve of RE, but they are developed and emphasised in a way which contributes to learning in RE.

For example, the ability to use a range of media to express ideas is particularly helpful in RE since it draws attention to the nature of the subject matter. The ideas, beliefs and values with which RE deals are best expressed not through analytical, descriptive prose, but through more imaginative, creative and subjective ways of expression. These may include the use of art, drama, music, movement and poetry. The ability to develop skills in these creative media will be learned through the curricular specialisms which deal with them, but the ability to use them in RE will enhance learning in the subject.

This is because, as we have previously noted, RE has an important subjective side to it which involves encouraging children to reflect upon what they are exploring. Reflection in this sense means the ability to ask subjective questions such as 'What is there of value in this for me?' and 'How does this change the way I look at things?'. The teacher of RE can help children in this process. Reflecting on one's own experiences and those of others requires time, patience and – a rare resource – quiet. An important part of the job of the RE teacher is to help children to ask the right questions, to avoid superficial responses, to look 'inwards' and as well as 'outwards' and to seek opportunities for reflection.

There is indeed a real sense in which the success of RE depends on the extent to which a teacher has been able to build up this reflective capacity in children.

Examples of the kind of skills emphasised in RE are given in Figure 15 below.

Knowledge

We have purposely left referring to knowledge until last in order to make the point that knowing facts (in RE or indeed in any other area of the curriculum) *cannot be separated from understanding*. Facts need to be placed in a context to have any meaning, and they are best assimilated by children through a developing understanding of concepts.

Let us take an illustration from another curriculum area. In an early version of the National Curriculum proposals for History there is a most helpful discussion of this point which needs to be carefully grasped in RE:

3.4 In order to know about, or understand, an historical event we need to acquire historical information but the constituents of that information – the names, dates and places – provide only the starting points for understanding. Without understanding, history is reduced to parrot learning and assessment to a parlour memory game. In the case of the French Revolution, the answer to the question 'What was the date of Louis XVI's execution?' may tell us something about the pupils' powers of recollection but nothing about their understanding of the great issues of social conflict, social change and the effect of the Revolution outside France. Such items of information are the building blocks upon which a true understanding of the event must be based.

3.5 In the study of history the essential objective must be the acquisition of knowledge as understanding. It is that understanding which provides the frame of reference within which the items of information, the historical facts, find their place and meaning. Knowledge as

GENERAL EDUCATIONAL SKILLS	EDUCATIONAL SKILLS EMPHASISED IN RELIGIOUS EDUCATION
The ability to …	The ability to …
<ul><li>communicate clearly in written and spoken words</li><li>listen attentively</li><li>co-operate with other pupils</li><li>observe, and use sources</li><li>gather and record information</li><li>present work in an organised manner.</li></ul>	<ul><li>use a range of media to express ideas</li><li>use periods of silence/stillness for reflection</li><li>use imagination to enter creatively into the motives, perceptions and attitudes of others</li><li>use technical terms of religion appropriately and correctly</li><li>use language appropriately to express emotions, opinions and values</li><li>acknowledge the basis of their own beliefs and values, and write/speak objectively about the beliefs and values of others</li><li>express their own thoughtful, personal responses to questions and issues about beliefs and values, using evidence and argument</li><li>discern and raise questions about those experiences which prompt religious and ethical responses to life</li><li>use empathy to understand why other people believe and behave as they do</li><li>apply the results of their exploration of religion and life-experiences to their own beliefs and values.</li></ul>

Figure 15 Skills in RE

understanding cannot be achieved without a knowledge of historical information, and the wider the base of information the greater the potential for developing understanding through the perception of significant connections and relationships. The learning of facts alone is not in itself sufficient for understanding.

3.6 While this is generally true of many branches of knowledge, history differs from most others in its central concern with the actions of people and the significance and consequences of those actions. Historical events cannot be understood without reference to the motives and beliefs of the participants, although there can be no absolute certainty why they acted as they did. Despite their professional concern for evidence and rigour, historians cannot therefore describe the past with the objectivity of natural scientists. They have to make a selection from the mass of evidence available and offer an interpretation of why and how events occurred as they did.

History for Ages 5 to 16, DES, July 1990

These comments could be applied with equal force to RE. RE is not a matter of acquiring a great mass of unconnected facts about religions. It is a process through which teachers select a limited range of information from the huge panorama of information available in order to help children perceive the connections between them and develop an understanding of the concepts which make sense of them. Of course some local authority Agreed Syllabuses will already have provided a selection of content from which teachers may choose appropriately in order to enhance children's understanding.

Thus we would see very little value in children simply knowing what is the third position of a *rakah*, who is excused from fasting, what is the name of the place where pilgrims throw stones, etc. They may learn such information quickly but

it is doubtful whether they will retain it all. That which is retained is very likely to be held in a very random way.

When we come to specifying the knowledge or information we are going to use in RE, we have to make a selection, and the selection is based on the concepts it is intended to inform. Let us suppose a Key Stage Three group are exploring a topic on the five pillars of Islam. They may gather an amazing array of facts about what Muslims do to observe these duties which will do little to advance their understanding of why Muslims behave in this way. The teacher, however, understanding that the five pillars are expressions of the concept of *ibadah* (worship) will make a selection from the great accumulation of possible information in order to help children understand this concept. The concept is illustrated through aspects of the five pillars.

Summary

In this section we have sought to achieve two things. Firstly, we have identified what we believe to be important concepts, attitudes and skills which teachers need to develop in children through their RE. Secondly, in discussing concepts, attitudes, skills and knowledge in that order, we have represented the style, balance and emphasis of the subject.

It is hoped that by being clear about this, teachers may arrive at a view not only of the nature of the subject but of how RE stands in relation to other areas of the curriculum. Thus it is intended that the specification of concepts, attitudes, skills and knowledge will contribute to both clearer thinking about continuity and progression in RE as well as providing pointers towards good practice in integrating RE, particularly in the primary school.

PART THREE

How can RE be planned?

So far we have established a principal aim, identified the source of content and examined some of the concepts, skills and attitudes with which the subject is concerned.

The task now is to see how the subject may be planned sequentially in such a way that it offers pupils a balanced programme which has variety, progression and relevance.

I Two sets of planning principles

It is acknowledged that there can never be one right programme of RE to be followed by all pupils in all schools. Many local and individual factors have to be considered when planning particular school programmes. There are, however, several important principles and guidelines which can be applied to the task of sequencing the teaching of the subject. The most important of these arises from an understanding of the way in which children in the classroom develop in their abilities to understand and reflect upon the material they are exploring. The second emerges when the logic of the field of enquiry is related to these understandings of the ways in which children learn.

Pupils and planning

The development of our understanding of the subject has made only slight reference to the question of what might be appropriate for primary, middle or secondary school pupils in RE. Many of the examples and ideas given so far might be quite unsuitable for five or ten year-olds, and others would be inappropriate for older children.

RE, like any other subject, depends on an understanding of the fact that teaching must be related to the ability of the children and their appropriate stage of development. In broad terms it is well established that children learn in different ways at different ages, but that it is not possible to relate age to learning development with any precision. It is also recognised that development is not uniform and that there are wide variations in ability between children of the same age. We are therefore well advised to speak only in general terms and to draw broad conclusions about where emphasis should be placed with any given group of children. The emphasis on broad, general categories applies as much to the moral and emotional development of children as it does to their intellectual development. Since RE is not simply a cognitive academic exercise, the teacher of RE needs to bear all these factors in mind in planning the subject.

We may describe in these general terms three broad stages of learning development through which children in the age range five to sixteen will pass. In the earliest years children will begin to form concepts through their own experience of the world around them. Later, they will begin to broaden their concepts through observation and by gathering and organising information. When they reach adolescence they will be able to use and apply concepts and general principles. These stages are not discreet but merge into each other, so that it is probably best to think in terms of where the emphasis needs to be placed rather than making sharp distinctions at particular ages. Figure 16 below illustrates this general distribution of emphasis.

This general scheme for recognising the kind of development of children's understanding which we might expect in RE can be expressed in terms of the way children might explore the subject's field of enquiry at the four main stages of schooling. This is shown in Figure 16.

Infant and Key Stage One

Infants and Key Stage One children will begin their RE through exploring their own experiences in relation to some of the key topics of shared human experience. They will be encouraged to reflect on their own feelings of pleasure, pain, awe, wonder, mystery, beauty. They will need to find ways of expressing those feelings through

movement, music, art. This will provide opportunity for stimulating their imagination. Their curiosity about their own feelings and about people, objects, places and events around them will develop. They will ask questions, some simple, some profound, and they will be encouraged to go on asking questions rather than arriving at solutions.

Some children will have their own experiences of religious groups and activities. They will be encouraged to explore their own experiences and those of others. To begin with, their exploration will be simply at the level of their own sensory perception. They will become aware that there are certain people, objects, buildings, places, forms of dress, foods, occasions and events that have special importance. They will begin to make simple identifications. The use of story will be important at this stage as a way of arousing their curiosity, encouraging the use of their imagination, and helping them to reflect on their own experience. Stories at this level may be drawn from the religious traditions, so that children may become familiar with them. Gradually children will begin to recognise and explore the differences between themselves and

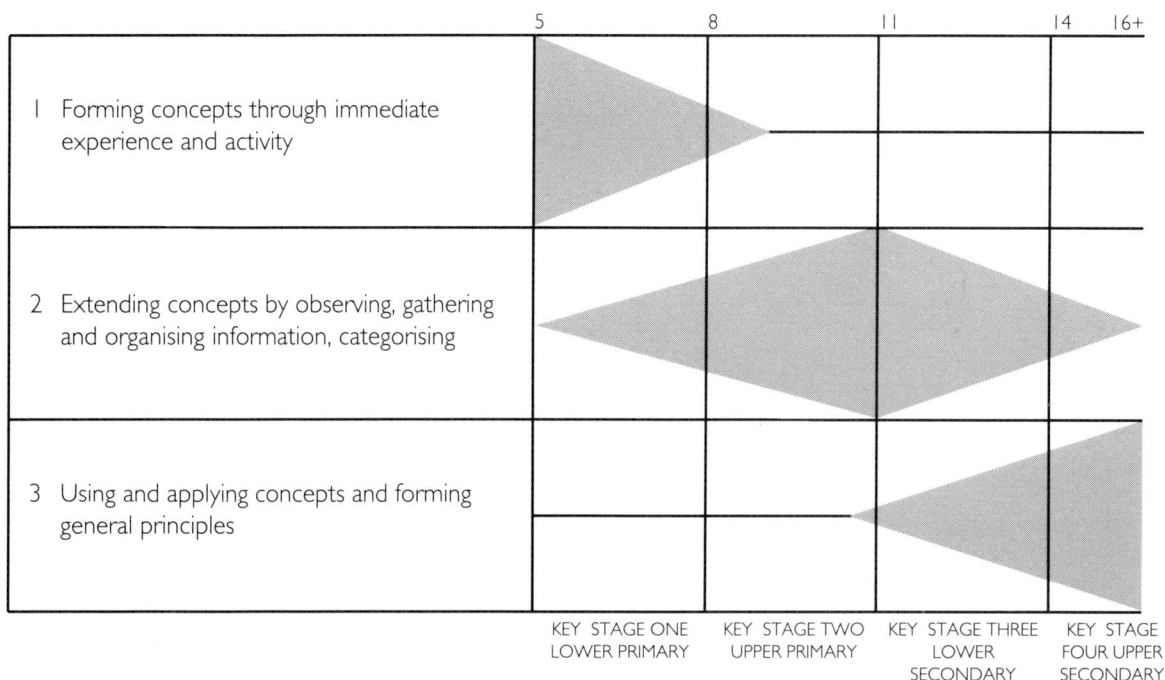

Figure 16 Exploring the RE field of enquiry at different levels

others. The foundations of relationship skills are laid when children are encouraged to accept and value both themselves and these differences, and at the same time to recognise and celebrate a common bond between all people.

The sequence of RE teaching at this stage is not of prime importance. Many of the elements may appear to an adult mind to be confusing and disjointed. The RE, however, can and should be planned in such a way that children are helped to explore as wide a range as possible of those elements of the subject which will later provide a foundation for further exploration. The actual organisation of the subject can be made easier where, for example, the assembly is seen as a way of stimulating children to explore further some of the experiences it deals with; and where topics chosen by the teachers collectively for theme work are of the kind that open up some of those more significant human experiences which are part of the subject's field of enquiry.

Key Stage Two

At this stage children are no longer dependent on their own sensory perceptions and are able to view other people in a more objective and detached way. The emphasis will be on gathering information, especially in relation to those topics which are significant for RE. They will begin to observe relationships between religious activities and to organise and categorise the information they gather. They will begin to use technical terminology and will be able to state beliefs in a simple way. They will need little encouragement to widen their own horizons, observing the way people behave, and exploring their reasons for doing so. They will still find it difficult to appreciate the feelings and experiences of other religious believers; but they may begin to form more coherent ideas of what it means to belong to particular religious traditions, especially through the use of biographical material.

Of special importance at this stage is the development of communication skills which will later help towards a more mature understanding of religion and avoid some of the pitfalls of literalism. Children will explore at a simple level

the way language is used to convey religious ideas – how, for example, metaphors are used to describe God, or how stories are told to explain the origins of the world. They will give close attention to the way in which religions use symbols, dramatic rituals, music and art to convey important ideas.

They will also widen the horizons of their understanding of significant human experience, and in particular, begin to see immediate, personal and local questions as aspects of wider, more universal ones. They will identify and make their own responses to some of the problems of being human. They will be encouraged to develop further their ability to ask and pursue more perceptive questions. They will also at this stage become familiar with some of the rules which are used in religion to guide behaviour. This will prepare the ground for a later consideration of how systems of rules and values apply to particular issues in the modern world.

Key Stage Three

This stage is not to be sharply distinguished from Key Stage Two, and the work done at lower secondary level will be a direct progression of work already undertaken. Thus pupils will continue to develop larger and more comprehensive categories for the material they explore, and will begin to develop the necessary concepts for handling it. In particular, they will explore the beliefs that underlie religious practice and start to draw them together in a coherent pattern. This is an appropriate stage for pupils to begin to build up a framework of understanding of particular religions, viewing them as a whole, and being able to relate behaviour, experience and belief to each other. They will begin to understand, for example, how a variety of different rituals all point towards a central core of beliefs and values, and how these in turn shape and inform basic attitudes to life.

They will at this stage continue to develop their understanding of the aesthetic and symbolic elements in religion. It is also an appropriate stage for children to begin their critical appraisal of some of the facts they have been studying. This will apply not only to rules and codes of behaviour, but also to basic beliefs and attitudes. They will need to sharpen their ability to raise perceptive questions and, in particular, to discuss them constructively with others.

They will now be able to think more deeply about the experience of being human. They will be able to distance this experience further from their own immediate concerns and to think in more abstract terms. Thus they will begin to acquire some understanding of basic concepts which underlie questions (e.g. authority, destiny) and some of the concepts which underlie religious belief (e.g. faith, salvation, non-attachment), so that at a later stage they will be able to perceive the interrelationships which lie at the heart of the subject. These concepts will, however, continue to be acquired through concrete examples.

Key Stage Four

By this stage pupils should be developing more general principles by being able to use and apply the concepts they have acquired, again based on concrete examples. There will be very much less emphasis on collecting basic information and much more on promoting understanding of inner beliefs and attitudes. In particular, pupils will begin to perceive how religious beliefs and attitudes are closely interrelated with those human experiences which raise ultimate questions. They may now begin to gain understanding of the distinctive features of religious and secular perspectives.

Throughout their RE programme they will have recognised the variety of ways in which religious practices and beliefs are expressed. They will now begin to recognise some of the varieties of interpretation and attitude found within religions, e.g. traditional and progressive/radical. This understanding is important, for it is in the upper secondary school that questions of relevance become central to the pupils' concerns. That is why RE at this stage will focus attention particularly on personal and social moral issues which are seen to be of concern and relevance.

They also provide one of the best ways for exploring the subject at this level. The issues are explored in RE to help pupils to perceive the ultimate questions they raise and to relate them to some of the varieties of beliefs and teachings of the traditional belief systems. This will also help them in the task of understanding some of the general principles which lie behind rules of behaviour and codes of conduct.

Key Stage Four pupils will be encouraged to evaluate for themselves the beliefs, attitudes and experiences they are exploring. The emphasis will be on developing criteria for critical judgement and sharpening their ability to get to the heart of issues. This should lead not only to an awareness of and respect for the way in which others behave and view life, but also to an understanding of the need for them to develop their own set of beliefs and values and a consistent style of life.

Continuing education

The level and breadth of understanding that might be achieved by the age of sixteen is intended to provide a foundation for continuing education – both the informal learning of the school leaver and the formal learning of the tertiary stage. School leavers should have sufficient knowledge and understanding of religion to recognise and respond to those aspects which might be encountered anywhere at any time, and sufficient awareness to continue to raise questions about, and reflect upon, their own experiences and those of others.

Those who are going on to pursue Religious Studies at a more advanced level will of course have the same basis of knowledge, understanding and awareness for themselves, but they should also have a firm and broad foundation on which to build their future studies. At the tertiary level it is most likely that their areas of study will take them into the exploration of aspects and perspectives which they have not really touched upon so far. Some of these will involve study in greater depth, others in greater breadth.

At the tertiary stage, therefore, we can expect that traditional belief systems will be explored, for example, in terms of the study of their historical development, or of a detailed study of sacred texts. Both these aspects, which have played a considerable part in RE in the primary and secondary phases in the past, are in fact much more appropriate to the tertiary level, since they involve handling language, concepts and varieties of interpretation which are beyond the understanding of younger children. Their studies might also involve them in exploring the psychological, political, sociological and cultural functions of religion. On a broader spectrum, their RE in the primary and secondary schools should provide the groundwork for exploring such aspects as the dialogue of faiths and the philosophy of religion.

Appropriate topics within the field of enquiry

Throughout the above discussion reference has been made both to what children can learn and to how they might learn it at different stages in their development.

When planning a programme of RE and setting it out in terms of a school syllabus, the emphasis should be on what is to be learned. In other words the syllabus should give a clear indication of the subject matter to be explored at each stage of schooling. Taken together across the whole 5–16 range, this should indicate the way in which children are helped to explore the total field of enquiry in appropriate ways. To achieve this progressive exploration, teachers need to combine this understanding of the logical structure of the field of enquiry with their insights into the ways in which children learn.

Reference to the RE field of enquiry in Figure 11 on page 24 will remind us that there are both observable and underlying aspects of each of the three sources of content and that any understanding of the relationships between these three sources involves grappling with complex and abstract concepts. The outer segments in each circle point to very concrete and observable events and behaviour. The inner circles and the interconnecting arrows suggest far more abstract

ideas and experiences. When this is linked to the fact that most people learn by progressing from the concrete to the abstract, a self-evident sequencing pattern emerges. RE begins with the observable features of religion and human experience and moves towards those abstract cores of ultimate questions, beliefs and spirituality.

This pattern of sequencing subject matter drawn from the subject's field of enquiry can be refined a little further if we take account of another general principle enunciated above. Children's learning is enhanced when they are helped to relate new knowledge to what is already familiar and within their present experience and comprehension.

The family context is familiar to the majority of children and thus provides a natural reference point to which they can relate new and unfamiliar patterns of behaviour, including those which reflect different religious beliefs. Examples drawn from these segments make very appropriate topics for lower primary pupils. At Key Stage One, pupils can also begin to use their experience of the school as a small community to relate to information about unfamiliar religious communities.

Reference to very individualistic behaviour patterns can be added during Key Stage Two. Topics which reflect the ways in which religious people relate their beliefs to public life can be introduced in the lower secondary years at Key Stage Three. These can continue into the upper secondary years when direct study of beliefs and spirituality should also be undertaken.

On this basis we can now set out in Figure 17 a viable sequencing pattern for planning an RE syllabus across the 5–16 age range. Only two of the circles are used because, as previously stressed, the remaining one points to pupils' and teachers' own individual patterns of belief and behaviour and therefore its inclusion cannot be planned into the curriculum. Material from these sources can only emerge in an ad hoc way within the context of particular lessons.

These diagrams are not, of course, meant to represent an inflexible pattern of progression.

They are intended primarily to suggest where emphasis should be placed in planning. Primary children will certainly be raising ultimate questions and thinking about beliefs, and upper secondary pupils may well be exploring aspects of the family context. The diagrams indicate where the emphasis is most appropriately placed.

Key Stage One In the lower primary aged band, topics arising from concrete and immediate happenings and experiences in the context of family and community life, including religious life would seem to be most appropriate.

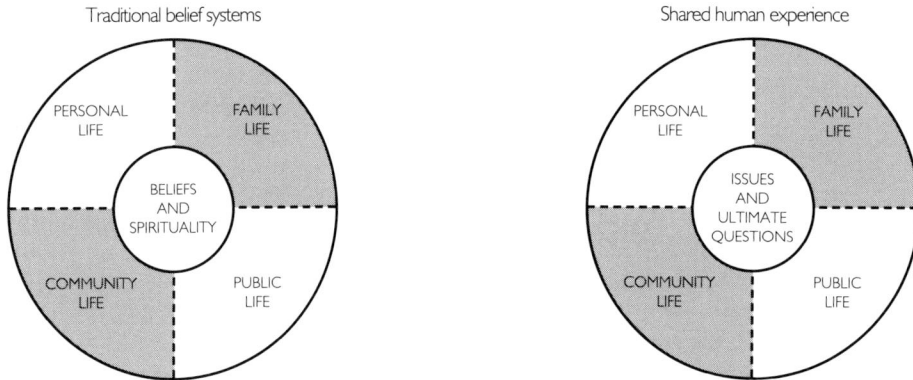

Traditional belief systems

Shared human experience

PERSONAL LIFE · FAMILY LIFE · BELIEFS AND SPIRITUALITY · COMMUNITY LIFE · PUBLIC LIFE

PERSONAL LIFE · FAMILY LIFE · ISSUES AND ULTIMATE QUESTIONS · COMMUNITY LIFE · PUBLIC LIFE

Key Stage Two Topics which focus on very personal and individual behaviour and values may be added for children in the upper primary years. By this time their natural self-centredness may have been lessened sufficiently to allow a more objective consideration of such topics.

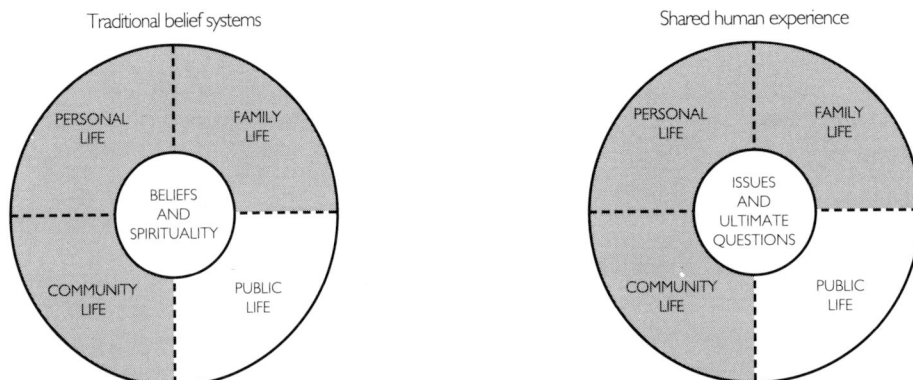

Traditional belief systems

Shared human experience

PERSONAL LIFE · FAMILY LIFE · BELIEFS AND SPIRITUALITY · COMMUNITY LIFE · PUBLIC LIFE

PERSONAL LIFE · FAMILY LIFE · ISSUES AND ULTIMATE QUESTIONS · COMMUNITY LIFE · PUBLIC LIFE

Key Stage Three In the lower secondary years many pupils will be ready to expand this diet to include topics which focus attention on the world community. They may also begin to study some of the ways in which the various belief systems relate central beliefs and values to public life, social structures and international issues.

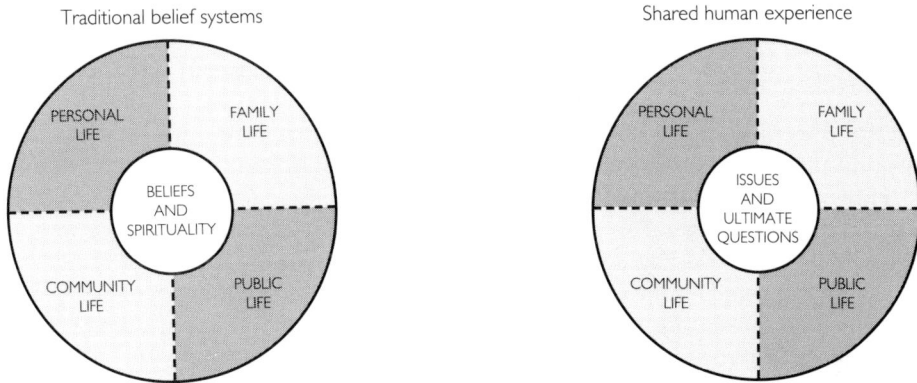

Traditional belief systems

Shared human experience

Key Stage Four By the time pupils reach the upper secondary levels, they should be ready to deepen their understanding of the ways in which central beliefs and values relate to public life, social structures and international issues. They should also be ready to explore ultimate questions and particular sets of beliefs and values in a more direct way. They may also be interested in examining in some detail and depth, the relationships between the three areas of content as shown.

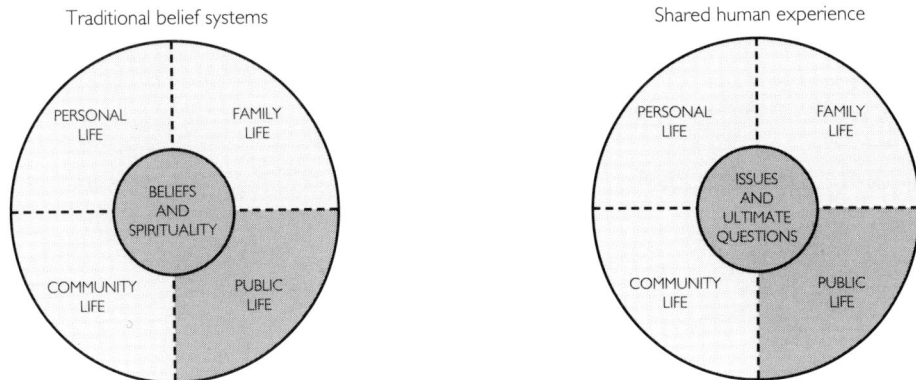

Traditional belief systems

Shared human experience

Figure 17   Areas of emphasis at different levels

2 Two approaches to planning

Over recent years two quite distinct, yet interrelated approaches to the teaching of RE in schools have been developed. Both of these approaches are valid and useful ways of exploring the subject's field of enquiry and for achieving its general aims and specific objectives.

A well-balanced programme of RE will give children opportunities to learn from both approaches. However, it is essential that in planning and presenting learning experiences, teachers are quite clear about the nature and purpose of each approach and about which one is being followed in any teaching situation. A failure to distinguish between the two almost inevitably results in confused teaching and muddled understanding on the part of pupils. The different objectives of the two approaches are important, since they will clearly determine the way in which relevant content is selected and used.

The systems approach

In this approach to the subject, the focus of attention is on just one of the systems. Children are being helped to develop an understanding of, for example, Christianity. Of course, there is no suggestion that the totality of the system is being explored under one particular topic – not even the whole school programme could provide sufficient time for that. The topic should deal with one particular aspect of the system, and not simply provide a springboard for leaping off onto other aspects. The systems approach does, however, enable the teacher to plan for a

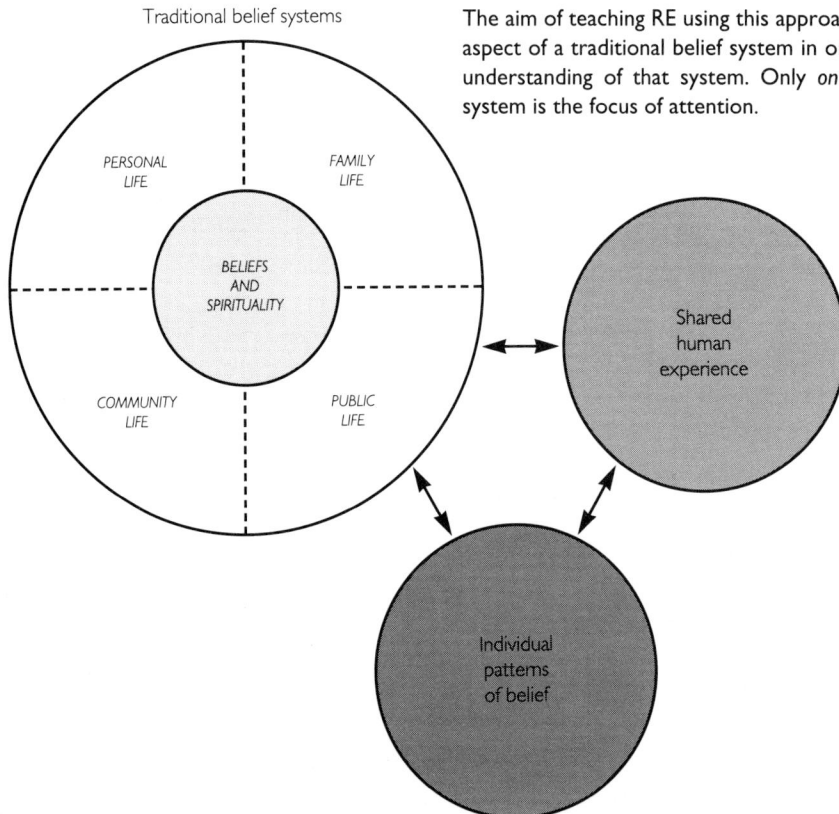

The aim of teaching RE using this approach is to explore an aspect of a traditional belief system in order to develop an understanding of that system. Only *one* traditional belief system is the focus of attention.

Figure 18   Using the systems approach

gradual building up by the children of a reasonably comprehensive picture of a particular system.

Although the main focus under this approach is on one particular system, the nature of the subject demands that links should be made with shared human experience and with the ideas and experiences of the children in the classroom. This should not be done in a merely artificial way. The aspect of human experience should arise clearly and centrally from the aspect of the traditional belief system under consideration. This aspect of human experience should in turn provide a link with the children's own concerns and experiences.

Let us take, for example, lessons dealing with Christian baptism using the systems approach. Various aspects of this topic can be dealt with in both the primary and the secondary school. Since we are following the systems approach the main and essential focus of the work will be on building up an understanding of the various practices and beliefs associated with baptism. This in turn, along with a range of other topics on other aspects of Christianity, will help children gradually to build up their understanding of Christianity as a whole.

Work on the topic of baptism may explore some of the rituals, symbols and stories associated with this practice, the roles, intentions and experiences of the participants and the Christian beliefs and values which underlie it. At the same time, there are a number of important themes which arise from a consideration of baptism and which help to relate this specifically Christian practice with wider human experiences and questions. For example, the themes of welcoming, belonging, responsibility, commitment, identity and hope all represent important dimensions of the practice of baptism and point to the links with human experiences. Some of the links may be more appropriately explored at primary level, others at secondary level. At the lower primary level, for example, the theme of welcoming may be dominant.

At the same time, pupils in the classroom will not simply be exploring the topic and its related themes as a detached, objective piece of study.

For some, the actual practices of baptism will be part of their own experience and awareness. They may have seen or participated in a baptism service, and may have their own unique perceptions of it. For others, baptism will appear strange and unfamiliar. For all of them, however, the themes and the questions they raise will provide material for reflecting on their own experiences, and the ideals, beliefs and values associated with Christian baptism will provide one of the sources through which they will refine their own beliefs and values.

It is not necessary for these links to be carefully and elaborately worked out and dwelt upon at every level. The stages by which the links are made are progressive and it is only at the upper secondary stage, at the earliest, where the nature of the links is explored in its own right. Thus, while the links remain throughout the RE curriculum, the essential focus of the systems approach is on the understanding of one particular system.

The life themes approach

A topic dealt with under this approach will focus quite clearly on helping children to explore and understand an aspect of human experience. In this case the teacher may draw upon quite a range of examples in order to illustrate and illuminate the topic. As a topic appropriate to RE it will have potential for raising ultimate questions and for that reason there will be important links with the traditional belief systems. For it is these systems whose beliefs, values and practices serve to interpret, support and challenge human experience and the questions it raises.

In most cases, therefore, the illustrations which are chosen to illuminate the topic will be drawn from the traditional belief systems. These will need to be set alongside other illustrations drawn from more general human experience in order to highlight the meaning and importance of the topic. The emphasis here is on variety. It therefore follows that illustrations drawn from traditional belief systems will reflect this variety.

Shared human experience

PERSONAL
LIFE

FAMILY
LIFE

Traditional
belief
systems

BELIEFS
AND
SPIRITUALITY

COMMUNITY
LIFE

PUBLIC
LIFE

Individual
patterns
of belief

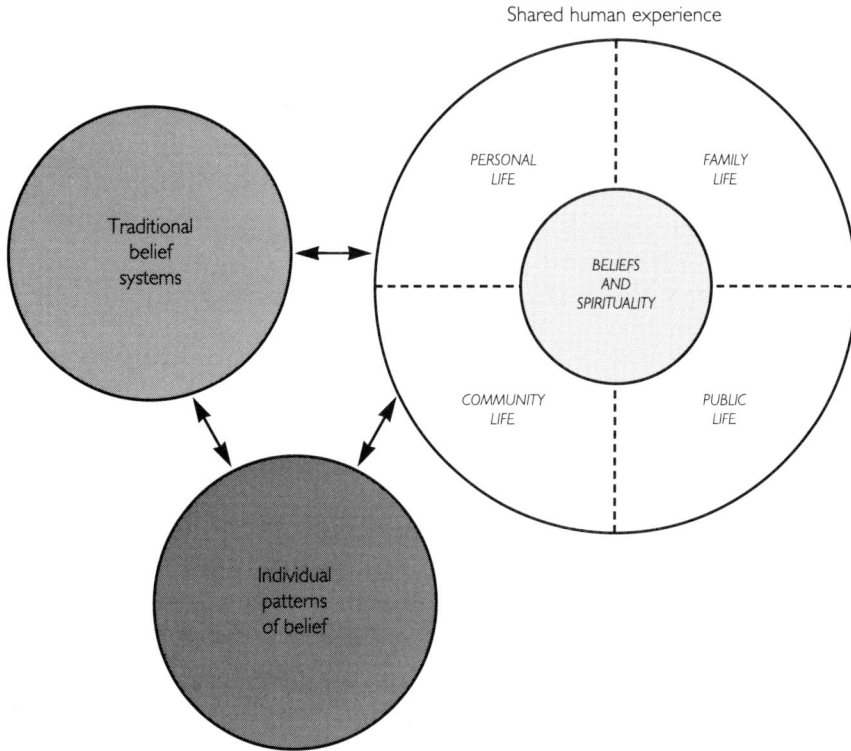

Figure 19 Using the life themes approach

In other words the topic should be illustrated from the beliefs and practices of more than one of the systems.

A sample theme

Let us take as an example work which might be done on the theme of 'caring'. The theme has good potential for RE since it opens up important questions about meaning and value. The theme is suitable at both primary and secondary levels. Children might begin to develop their under-standing of the theme by considering ways in which others care for them and how the care is shown, gradually widening their understanding by exploring other examples – caring for the sick, lonely or poor, the way communities care for one another, organised and informal caring. There are clear links with traditional belief systems and examples of different forms of caring will be drawn from various traditions – the *langar* as an expression of the caring work of the Sikh community, or the way in which Muslims care for the poor in their communities through the distribution of *zakat*, or the example of Christian caring found in the work of Mother Teresa of Calcutta.

At the secondary level, the same theme may be explored by using other concrete examples to raise some of the issues related to the theme of 'care'. Why should we care? What is the best way to show care? Is justice better than charity? Who is my neighbour? Illustrations from traditional belief systems should demonstrate the different ways in which they serve to interpret, support and challenge the human experience of the need for caring – values such as love and compassion, and ideas such as the belief that God cares.

As with the systems approach the concern is not

merely to examine and study what is 'out there' but to help children to look at some of the questions and implications of the human experience of caring for themselves and for their own values, beliefs and style of life. Thus in this approach also there are important links between the three areas of the field of enquiry. The emphasis, however, in the life themes approach is on developing our understanding of the theme and of the questions and issues it raises, not on learning about particular traditional belief systems. In this case the concrete examples (Mother Teresa, *zakat* and the *langar*) are introduced in order to broaden the concept of caring; not to study the wider beliefs and practices of Sikhism, Islam and Christianity.

Distinctions between the two approaches

The difference between the two approaches should be apparent from the examples already given above. It does mean that a common topic could be included in both a systems approach and a life themes approach, but the purpose of its inclusion and the way it is used in the classroom will differ.

The topic of baptism is a case in point. In a systems approach what is important is the way in which an exploration of the topic helps towards an understanding of Christianity. In a life themes approach, however, baptism might appear in a number of contexts by way of illustration, depending on the theme chosen. For example, a theme of 'welcoming' could include reference to baptism as an example. What is being explored here is the way in which welcoming a new child is expressed in the baptism of infants. What is *not* being explored is all the detail of the service, the symbols used, the people who participate, or the Christian beliefs that underlie the service, *unless* they are material to the theme of welcome.

In contrast, another theme such as responsibility could include a reference to baptism as an illustration. In this case, the emphasis of the exploration would be firmly on the promises made by the parents and the way in which the

service serves to heighten their awareness of their responsibility for loving and nurturing a newborn child. Other aspects of the service may be material to the theme – the responsibility of the community to support the family, for example – but the purpose of the exercise is to focus attention on the way Christians interpret *responsibility*, not on the details of the baptism service.

At the same time, the Christian interpretation of responsibility expressed in the baptism service will be just one example amongst others. We might include an example from Buddhism – the responsibility of the laity to maintain the *sangha*; and one from Judaism – the responsibility of children to care for their parents in old age, expressed through the particular example of an extended Jewish family. In all cases, the purpose of the exercise is not to explore the details of Christian, Buddhist or Jewish practice, but to illuminate the theme of responsibility, the ultimate questions it raises, and some of the responses that are given to these questions.

Avoiding confusion

Careful regard to the distinctions between the two approaches will avoid some of the confusions that could arise. These are most common where a theme (such as 'welcome') touches on the example (such as 'baptism') but then goes on to explore other aspects of that example in detail, rather than concentrating on the theme.

The danger of this kind of confusion is very obvious in the attempts of some teachers to deal with religions thematically; that is, to organise teaching on the basis of themes which appear to be common to all or most religious traditions (pilgrimage, worship, festivals, etc.). We suspect that this approach usually distorts the traditions and does little to develop children's understanding of the subject. It is far better to be quite clear which approach is being used, and therefore to be clear what the objective of exploring the topic is really supposed to be. Thus it is better to be specific and deal with pilgrimage in Islam, or Christians celebrating Holy

Communion, or a Jewish family at Passover time as topics under the systems approach, in order to build up an understanding of Islam or Christianity or Judaism. On the other hand, a topic such as celebration could be used under the life themes approach. The purpose of this topic would be to explore and raise questions about the human capacity to celebrate, the way in which people and events are highly valued, and how people express their joy and identity together. Passover, Easter, Ramadan, Diwali could then furnish examples of celebration, but only to illuminate the theme and the questions, not to provide a lead into explaining particular religions.

Application at different levels

It may be useful to draw together the basic principles of the stages of children's development and the two approaches to RE, and to clarify them by taking example topics.

	POSSIBLE CONTENT	LINKS WITH SHARED HUMAN EXPERIENCE	LINKS WITH INDIVIDUAL PATTERNS OF BELIEF
LOWER PRIMARY KEY STAGE ONE	**Sharing** in a simple *Seder* meal – **becoming familiar** with the dry **taste** of *matzah*, the bitter taste of herbs, the sweet taste of *charoset* – **hearing the story** of Passover night – **singing** some of the songs used on this occasion – **listening** to the young children's **questions** – **playing** at finding the *afikomen*	Enjoying important occasions together	What I have to share and enjoy
UPPER PRIMARY KEY STAGE TWO	**Finding out** about *chametz* – **learning the details** of the Seder meal, and the order of the various parts – **acting the roles** of the various members of the family – **exploring the meanings** given to each of the special foods and the cups of wine – **finding out** about other aspects of the Passover celebrations – **reading** the story of the Exodus	Following customs Conveying meaning through symbols	Customs that are important to me
LOWER SECONDARY KEY STAGE THREE	**Exploring** important Jewish **beliefs** (expressed in the Passover celebrations) – e.g. The Chosen People (the *Haggadah*); the *Torah* (*Mitzvoth* relating to Passover); the Messiah (Elijah's cup) – **recognising** important Jewish **values** (the family); **understanding concepts**, e.g. tradition (reliving the past)	Keeping rules Sharing beliefs about ourselves and the world we live in	Rules and beliefs I live by
UPPER SECONDARY KEY STAGE FOUR	**Understanding the importance** for Jews of their sense of identity (noting some cultural variations in the celebration of Passover); **exploring the reasons** why freedom is so important to Jews (related to the prayers for persecuted Jews); **appreciating** Jewish hopes and aspirations for the future ('next year in Jerusalem').	Celebrating freedom Hoping in the future	What makes me free? What do I hope for?

Figure 20   An example of the systems approach Topic: Passover

44

The example in Figure 20 relates to the topic of Passover which is explored according to the systems approach. The example in Figure 21 below is a consideration of belonging following the life themes approach.

The emphasis in each example is focused on what may be explored, i.e. the kind of content that might be suitable at the different stages of development. In each case possible links with the other areas of the field of enquiry are given as suggestions.

The examples given here suggest not only the kind of content which could be used at each of the age levels, but also some of the processes which might be appropriate to encourage learning. The relevant processes are suggested in each case by the words in italics. The links with the other areas of the field of enquiry arise directly out of the content and processes, and are not merely incidental to them. At the same time it is important to remember that the links are illustrative. They are certainly not the only possible examples of links. But the main focus in both approaches is on the basic content. Thus it can be seen clearly that the purpose of the work done under the systems approach is to learn more about and build up an understanding of Judaism and the purpose of the teaching and learning under the life themes approach is to

	POSSIBLE CONTENT	LINKS WITH TRADITIONAL BELIEF SYSTEMS	LINKS WITH INDIVIDUAL PATTERNS OF BELIEF
LOWER PRIMARY KEY STAGE ONE	**Sharing** some of the important things that belong to us – **talking** about some of the special people/groups that we belong to – **singing songs** expressing the happiness of belonging – **thinking about** ways in which other people love, care for and protect us – listening to stories on these themes	**Stories** illustrating the themes e.g. Guru Nanak and his friends; the prodigal son; Gautama's journey from his palace; Uncle Abu Talib; **Songs** – e.g. *Shalom Havarim*	What helps me feel secure? Who do I belong to? How can I show that I belong?
UPPER PRIMARY KEY STAGE TWO	**Finding out about** the great diversity of families, groups and societies to which people belong – **exploring categories** of belonging in terms of importance – **learning** some of the distinctive **features** of particular groups (dress, behaviour, customs) – **considering the meaning** of 'being British'	**Finding out** what it means to belong to, e.g. a Jewish family (special rules about food), or local Sikh community (dress), or the Christian Church (obligations)	Who do I belong to most? Why am I different?
LOWER SECONDARY KEY STAGE THREE	**Exploring what it means** to belong in terms of rules, norms, values, constraints, possibilities; **understanding what it means** to belong to socially unacceptable groups – and what it feels like to have no sense of belonging	**Exploring** different kinds of group rules, e.g. rules associated with caste; the Five Pillars of Islam; the Precepts of Buddha; (also, e.g. the 227 rules of the *Vinaya*)	Whose 'group rules' do I follow? How important are these rules to me?
UPPER SECONDARY KEY STAGE FOUR	**Considering examples** of conflicts of loyalty within groups – **appreciating** how belonging to a group shapes one's sense of **identity** and **awareness** of those who belong to other groups – understanding the ways in which **beliefs influence** groups.	**Considering ideas** of inclusion and exclusivism, e.g. in Islam and Christianity: **tensions** experienced by, e.g. Sikhs in British culture	What are my values? What conflicts of loyalty am I aware of? How can I resolve them? What do I believe about people who belong to other groups/societies?

Figure 21   An example of the life themes approach Topic: Belonging

explore what it means to belong, and to build up an understanding of the concept of identity.

With this distinction in mind, the basic guidelines about how the example links are used become clearer. For instance, the links with traditional belief systems under the theme of belonging show that variety in the examples is important. It is not the prime task here to build up detailed understanding of the various traditions, but rather to provide varied examples of what it means to belong. Thus, at the upper primary level, finding out what it means to belong to a Jewish family, a local Sikh community and the Christian Church provides a variety of examples of belonging. Distinctive features of a Jewish family might be explored through the concrete example of dietary rules. Distinctive features of a local Sikh community might be explored through the concrete example of dress, and so on. The purpose of these illustrations is not to focus attention on the details of them, nor on their wider ramifications for the communities in question, but to illustrate different features at different levels and within different contexts to which people belong.

Similarly, at the lower secondary level, the illustrations given are designed to provide varied examples of different kinds of group rules. Some have to do with, for example, 'who you can mix with' or 'who you can marry' (caste rules). Others are very general, and concern basic principles for one's whole life (the Five Pillars of Islam or the Precepts of the Buddha – which provide an interesting contrast). Others are very detailed (the 227 rules followed by Buddhist monks). There is no question here of looking at the rules in great detail, or of understanding the place of the *sangha* in Buddhism, but simply of recognising that some people's sense of belonging is governed by very detailed and precise rules covering every aspect of a person's life.

The purpose of the links, therefore, is gradually to build up an understanding of the interrelationship between fundamental human experiences, concerns and questions on the one hand, and the basic ideas, beliefs, values and practices of traditional belief systems on the other hand. The emphasis, it will be noted, is on building up an understanding. In the earlier stages of schooling the links are there, but only implicitly as far as the children are concerned. They will usually not become explicit until children are much older. It is essential, however, that the teacher has a very clear grasp of the way in which the links operate. Such a conception on the part of the teacher is of paramount importance in understanding the structure of the subject, and therefore in planning how to teach it.

It has already been made clear that the examples of the two approaches given above are highly artificial. It is most unlikely that any teacher would consider dealing with these particular topics in such a methodically sequential fashion, nor is it desirable that they should do so. The examples do, however, help to illustrate the principle that anything may be taught at any age, provided that the structure of teaching and learning has been clearly grasped by the teacher. They also show the way in which the 'spiral curriculum' nature of RE can operate in practice. Broad general concepts and ideas are built up from limited concrete examples, and it is possible to use the same basic topic in a number of different ways at different levels of understanding.

A balanced programme

The two approaches we have considered represent different ways of exploring the RE field of enquiry. The emphasis so far has been very much on the differences between them. The whole point of the differences is to make clear that there are different intentions and objectives in each case, and that a clear understanding of the distinctions will help greatly when it comes to planning topics in RE.

At the same time, both these approaches remain faithful to the essential nature of the subject, for they enable relevant links to be made between the three areas of the field of enquiry. However, in an overall programme of RE, it is also essential that a balance is achieved between the two approaches. This balance is important for two reasons.

Firstly, although it is perfectly possible to plan a complete RE programme using just one approach, such a scheme is likely to distort the essential nature of the subject – and it is likely to lack the variety which is also an important ingredient in RE. A programme of RE restricted entirely to the systems approach may leave children with the impression that belief systems are really conglomerates of strange practices and unusual ideas followed by particular groups of people who happen to think them important. They may fail to see and experience something of the force and urgency of those aspects of human experience to which they relate.

On the other hand, a programme based entirely on the life themes approach has the obvious limitation that children are unlikely to develop a systematic conception of any traditional belief system. They may have a wide knowledge and sensitive appreciation of life's puzzles and mysteries. They will not have a clear and coherent understanding of some of the great belief systems which have inspired and challenged countless people for generations.

The second reason why balance is important has to do with the way in which children's understanding develops. In the youngest years of schooling, children learn primarily from their own immediate experiences and those of people around them. This suggests that some of the kind of themes which can be dealt with through the life themes approach will be most suitable for them. To begin with, there is no need for a carefully structured and systematic programme. This in fact accords well with the kind of approach to teaching in general which we find in most infant and lower primary classes.

The middle years of schooling are, for reasons already suggested, particularly suited to the gathering and organisation of information. This suggests that the systems approach can be especially helpful in these years as a means of building up children's knowledge and understanding of particular systems.

Towards the end of secondary schooling, when questions of meaning, application and relevance assume primary importance, it is likely that the life themes approach will be found most useful. It will also, of course, be the period of schooling where a more integrated understanding of the RE field of enquiry will be expected.

This overall pattern is a question of emphasis rather than strict linear development, as Figure 22 shows.

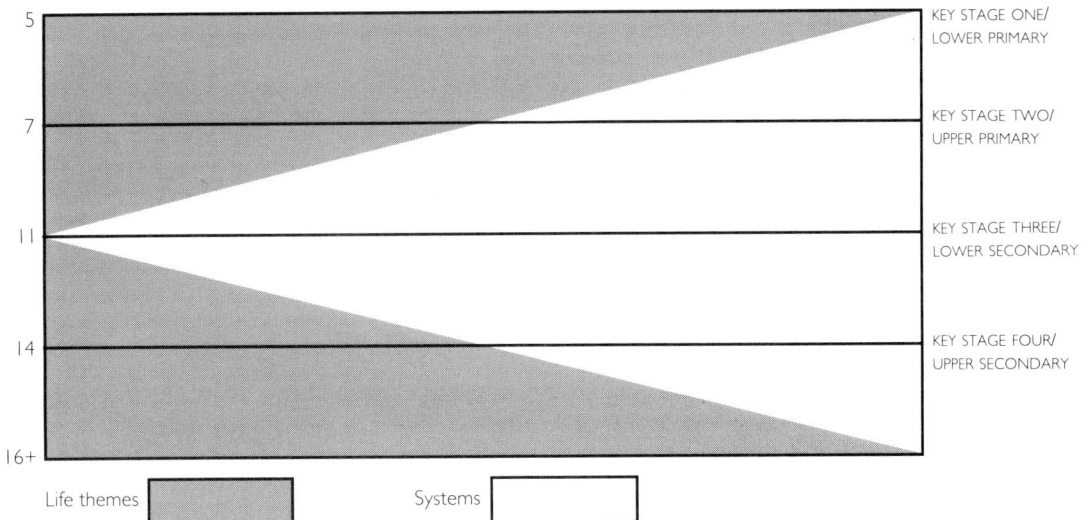

Figure 22 *Balance of emphasis in the use of systems/life themes approaches at different levels*

3 Identifying suitable topics

When teachers are planning their programme of RE, it is clear that they need to be able to break down the subject into manageable topics. This is necessarily an artificial exercise, but it can make a useful contribution to children's understanding. The basic principles for selecting material for RE, and for relating it to children's levels of understanding and ability, have already been considered.

It is important to recognise that there is no definitive list of topics that will fit the situation of every school. At the same time, the kind of topics which could usefully be covered in the classroom are suggested in the teacher's manuals, *Christianity*, *Islam* and *Judaism*. The purpose of this section is simply to reiterate some important points to consider in identifying topics.

Choosing the right topics

Any topic that is chosen must have potential for exploring an aspect of the subject's field of enquiry. It must be clear from the title of the topic which area of the field of enquiry is being explored, and which approach is being used.

For these reasons it is best to avoid stating topics purely in terms of the subject matter being considered. A title such as 'Holy Communion' is misleading. It gives no indication of what, precisely, children are to explore about Holy Communion. The same would apply to the title 'Poverty'.

For example, the title 'Sharing a special Christian meal' indicates more clearly that the experience of sharing is the focus of the topic, and that the purpose is not to explore in great detail what happens on this occasion. It is therefore an appropriate lower primary topic. On the other hand, the title 'Celebrating the Mass in a Roman Catholic church' suggests that we are looking at what happens in church, and looking at the details of the service. This would be a suitable upper primary topic. Alternatively, we could take the title 'What is a sacrament?' In this case we would be considering the concept of sacrament and using Holy Communion as an illustration. In each case Holy Communion is the subject matter but the different titles clearly indicate the level at which it is being explored and what aspect is being considered.

Similarly, titles such as 'What does it feel like to be poor?', 'Why are there poor people in the world?' and 'Attitudes to poverty' are far more indicative than simply using the word 'Poverty'.

As a further example of the importance of stating topics in a more precise form, we might refer back to the last section where we were considering the two approaches to RE using the general topics of 'Passover' and 'Belonging'. Neither of these, as titles, gives any real indication of what the exploration is intended to achieve. If, however, they are set out as shown in Figure 23 below, the intention becomes much clearer. This clarity makes the planning of the subject much more precise, allows for continuity and progression, and indicates what the subject

	SYSTEMS: PASSOVER	LIFE THEMES: BELONGING
Key Stage One	Enjoying Passover	We all belong to someone
Key Stage Two	Learning about the Seder meal	Learning about groups to which people belong
Key Stage Three	Exploring the meaning of Passover	What does it mean to belong?
Key Stage Four	The importance of Passover for Jewish people	Identity and belonging

Figure 23   Illustrating precise purpose in topics planned for exploration

is all about. Another reason for making topics as specific as possible is that it avoids the danger of allowing a topic to become a peg on which any apparently connected (and often unconnected) idea can be hung.

Topics and themes in the primary school

The last point is particularly pertinent to the situation of RE in the primary school. There is, of course, a very wide range of practice as far as the primary curriculum as a whole is concerned, and as far as RE itself is concerned. There are also certain attitudes among some primary teachers which militate against a well-planned and clearly structured RE programme.

In most primary schools, the day is divided between work on specific areas and theme work. The ratio of the two varies considerably. RE can and should form part of the specific 'subject' work that can be done in the primary school. This does not mean telling an unconnected story, unrelated to anything else that has happened, at the end of the day. There is plenty of material and there are suitable topics through which primary children from the age of five onwards begin to explore the RE field of enquiry.

RE may, of course, also be incorporated in theme work. Here, however, caution is necessary. A common pattern in primary schools is for a theme to be selected and then explored in a number of dimensions, such as mathematics, language, environmental studies, science, art and crafts, RE, personal development, etc. The key to this exercise is the choice of theme. If it is of any value, it should be a theme worth exploring in itself, for which the various dimensions provide illumination, and opportunities for exploration as well as skill development. If, however, the theme is not carefully chosen, teachers may be forced to bend the topic to fit the theme, or stretch the dimension of the theme to fit the topic, in ways which destroy the educational potential of both. RE is especially prone to this treatment.

The fact is that some themes are suitable for treatment in RE while others are not. Some have a high potential for fulfilling the aims and objectives of RE, others have a very low potential. Some examples may help to clarify this difficulty.

Themes such as 'myself', 'people who care' and 'harvest' have a relatively high potential for RE. They are themes which enable children to explore aspects of the subject's field of enquiry and which have potential, sooner or later, for opening up ultimate questions and matters of belief and value. Themes such as 'plants' or 'our neighbourhood' may have potential for RE, but it very much depends how they are handled. If the theme of 'plants' opens up questions about the wonder of the natural order, and if 'our neighbourhood' helps children to explore, for example, particularly important groups or buildings in the locality ('the local church', 'the mosque' etc.), then they have good potential for RE. On the other hand, themes such as 'farming' or 'transport' have very low potential for RE unless they are handled in a very subtle way by a very perceptive teacher – and the chances are that the subtlety will be quite lost on children.

Avoiding irrelevance

The great danger is that teachers may take some of these very low-potential themes and try to force some RE into them. That is why we still (occasionally, we hope) come across a consideration of Jesus as the Good Shepherd or the parable of the sower tucked into some rural theme and, worse still, transport in ancient Palestine or bullock-carts of the Bible as the RE element in 'transport'. The last two examples on transport are so completely irrelevant to the aims and objectives of RE as to be meaningless – and they have very little potential as history. The other two examples of the Good Shepherd and the sower as RE topics under 'farming' are slightly more subtle, but equally meaningless as RE. The point is that, in terms of their meaning, the notion of Jesus as the Good Shepherd and the parable of the sower have nothing whatsoever to do with 'farming'. The metaphor of 'Shepherd' has to do with 'leadership' and 'service' or 'care' and the idea of Jesus as the Good Shepherd could, possibly, be introduced if children were looking at those themes. The point of the parable of the sower is, in fact, fairly sophisticated, and depends on an understanding of the differences between parables and allegories.

There is, of course, no reason why young children should not hear the story of the sower. In this case they will simply be enjoying it as a story for the pleasure it gives and the impression it leaves. It is, however, much more appropriate to consider it under a heading such as 'stories Jesus told'; it may then be enjoyed in the same way as other stories told by other important religious leaders.

It is essential, therefore, that primary teachers are absolutely clear what they are trying to achieve in RE, so that they can see the relevance or otherwise of particular themes.

Planning an RE component

The introduction of attainment targets and programmes of study in the core and foundation subjects of the National Curriculum has high-lighted the fact that a single topic or theme may not always fulfil the aims and purposes of all the subjects of the curriculum. Therefore, education authorities and individual schools have worked on a variety of approaches to topic planning. This may result in some subjects being dealt with in one way, others in another. We believe that the same considerations need to be given to the nature of RE as to other subjects. Thus some topics may have no worthwhile RE dimension to them, and there is no point in trying to force such a topic into a mould in which it will not fit. It is much better, we would argue, to look at a quite separate RE topic that really helps to develop understanding.

The same general point also applies to primary practice in devising 'topic webs'. RE suffers in the same way when attempts are made to incorporate what is ostensibly RE material purely by word association with the theme in question. It is quite possible, simply by the process of word association, to move right away from the main topic so that some of the material being considered bears absolutely no meaningful relationship to the theme.

QUESTIONS ARISING OUT OF OUR SHARED HUMAN EXPERIENCE	EXAMPLES OF CONTENT TAKEN FROM TRADITIONAL BELIEF SYSTEMS	CROSS-CURRICULAR TOPIC
Natural World	Things people do at harvest time (Christian harvest; Jewish Sukkot)	Autumn
Celebrations	Special foods used in celebration (Christian Easter foods; Buddhist offering of food in *puja*)	Food
Lifestyles	Special things people do as a family (Muslim breaking fast during Ramadan; Christians attending church)	The family
Stages of Life	Ways of welcoming babies (Christian baptism, chrismation; Hindu shaving the head, naming)	Beginnings
Relationships	Ways of caring for others (Muslim *zakat*; Sikh *langar*)	Ourselves and others
Rules and Issues	Rules about what people wear (Sikh 5 Ks; Buddhist saffron robes)	Clothes
Suffering	Stories of losing valuable things (Buddhist Kisagotama; Jewish and Christian Job and his family)	Precious things

Figure 24 An approach to planning an RE component in topic work

It is partly because of this complexity, and the difficulty in identifying suitable themes, that the place of RE in the primary curriculum is sometimes recognised merely by an unrelated and unconnected story at the end of the day or by the excuses that 'we do it in assembly' or 'RE is going on all the time'. None of these is satisfactory. RE may legitimately be taught in its own right from the infant stage onwards, and it may be meaningfully incorporated in carefully chosen themes.

Figure 24 suggests one way in which teachers in the primary school may approach planning an RE component in topic work. The examples given relate closely to some of the life theme categories outlined in Figure 9 on page 22. The examples in Figure 24 indicate a conceptual link between the life themes categories in the first column and the general topic headings in the third column.

Thus in the first topic, Autumn, children will be able to explore aspects of the natural world through a number of curriculum areas. The question that the teacher of RE needs to ask, however, is 'What content taken from the RE field of enquiry would enable me to make meaningful conceptual links?' In this particular example the emphasis would be on the things that people do at harvest time. This would enable teacher and children to learn something about, for example, Christian harvest and Jewish *sukkot*. They would, however, also be able to explore and consider some of the important questions arising out of our shared human experience of the natural world: for example, 'What makes something grow?', 'Can the world produce enough food for all people?', 'Why is there hunger?'

By exploring such questions as these the teacher is able to make links with the examples of harvest celebrations. Thus an exploration of harvest celebrations from one or more of the traditional belief systems can raise further questions such as 'Is it important to say thank you for food?', 'Is it important to remember or thank God some-times?' At the same time, children will be helped to understand that people show their thanks in different ways.

The LEA Agreed Syllabus and the school context

As noted elsewhere in this manual the LEA Agreed Syllabus remains the legal basis of RE in any given authority. However, there are a number of important points that need to be recognised when considering the agreed syllabus in the context of the school and the classroom.

At the time of writing, a number of local authorities have issued new agreed syllabuses in response to the 1988 Education Reform Act. Some of these contain attainment targets and programmes of study for RE. Indeed most local authorities are considering the question of attainment through their Standing Advisory Councils for Religious Education. With the implementation of the 1988 Act, many LEA advisers for RE took the view that there were strong arguments in favour of RE adopting the basic structure of the National Curriculum. It was felt that it was important to give RE its proper status alongside other curriculum areas.

Of course the place of RE in the curriculum of each school will vary. There will be different styles of timetabling as well as a variety of approaches to curriculum planning which may include seeing RE as part of an integrated whole.

Whatever the case, it is important to point out that the three circle model described in this manual is not only suitable for use in planning RE in a variety of ways but also accords very closely with the most recent developments in local authority syllabus construction.

Another factor which will determine how RE is taught and, to some extent, what is taught will be the school's social context. The local context may well determine where the emphasis has to be placed. For example, it would follow that where 70 percent of the school population is Sikh, a study of Sikhism within the educational context of the school should feature prominently (but certainly not exclusively) in the RE programme.

The realities of the school's capitation and the way 'the cake is divided' will be a crucial matter in determining what can be included in the RE programme. This does not mean that there are indispensable resources, nor that the ingenious teacher cannot find ways of making something come alive for children without having access to the most sophisticated technology and techniques. It does recognise that the availability of resources is important and also that, in reality, good resources are often the point of departure for worthwhile curriculum development.

Finally, since the teacher is the most important resource available to the children, it is essential that the teacher of RE in the secondary school, and the subject co-ordinator in the primary school, have a clear understanding of what they are doing and why they are doing it. But no teacher can be an inexhaustible compendium of knowledge, and it is recognised that many of those who do teach the subject have not been trained for that purpose. While this is to be regretted, one has to recognise this constraint on the RE curriculum and work to the strengths of teachers, rather than their weaknesses. This must not, however, become an excuse for not allowing both the time and opportunity for teachers to develop new areas of expertise.

PART FOUR

How can RE be taught?

Our concentration so far has been on identifying and organising appropriate content in RE. This is entirely proper in a manual which claims to guide teachers towards a full understanding of the distinctive nature and purpose of RE as a subject in schools.

However, the quality of teaching, or the methods of directing pupil learning, adopted by teachers are crucial if the subject matter is to come alive and be processed by pupils in a way which genuinely contributes to their instruction.

Of course, very few teaching styles and methods are specific to any one subject. Wise teachers learn from each other, as well as from books, in order to expand their repertoire of creative and successful techniques for planning and presenting lessons and creating opportunities for learning.

In this section we offer some broad guidelines which will help the progression from the planning of the overall school programme in RE to the task of designing and presenting RE lessons which are consistent with the nature and aims of the subject and appropriate to the needs and interests of different groups of pupils in schools.

1 Designing units of work

There are several levels at which a subject in school may be planned and organised. As far as RE is concerned, this process actually starts outside school with the local authority's agreed syllabus. As we noted on page 51 some local authorities have responded to the Education Reform Act and the introduction of the National Curriculum by issuing a new agreed syllabus or a local document that sets out a structure for RE along the lines of National Curriculum principles. At the time of writing, the nature of the agreed syllabus varies between those that deal with very broad principles and those which prescribe attainment targets and programmes of study.

However, in all cases the agreed syllabus still requires translation into the individual school and classroom situation. Here the first stage of planning, logically, is the school's RE syllabus which presents an overview of the teaching of the subject right across the age range. The syllabus is then broken down into years and terms, where the general themes for these divisions can be set out. Within each year and term, a number of more specific topics will be covered, and these in turn will be broken down into lessons.

What is meant by a unit of work?

Ideally, the school syllabus will state, within each year, the topics to be covered. These will be set out in the kind of form suggested in Part Three of this book. The work on that topic may range over a number of lessons, in some cases only one or two, in others five or six. The number is not important. This series of lessons is referred to here as a unit of work. It is a short series of learning experiences which has a self-contained purpose and its own specific, short-term objectives, and which at the same time makes a contribution to the overall educational aim of the subject.

Thus, for example, a unit of work may be entitled 'Learning about the Seder meal'. The number of lessons needed to cover this topic will depend on the teacher's assessment of its importance within the overall syllabus, as well as on a range of other considerations. It is possible however that the unit of work could be broken down into two or three lessons covering different aspects, or exploring the topic in different ways. There is no one right way of setting out the details of a particular unit of work for pupils in schools.

The one offered below contains the essential characteristics suggested in the definition and provides an effective means for communicating to other teachers what the unit is all about and how it might be taught in different situations.

The discipline of designing all units of work within the school programme, in a format such as the one offered here, not only provides a useful guide to all teachers involved in the programme but ensures that the RE curriculum is clearly structured, developmental without being repetitive, and accessible for close scrutiny and regular evaluation and improvement.

Approach

In the previous chapter we outlined two different, though related, approaches to the task of planning units of work in RE: the systems and life themes approaches. Each approach has its own distinctive emphasis, mixture of content drawn from the total field of enquiry, and its own purpose in relation to the general aim of the subject.

When designing particular units of work it is essential that teachers are clear in their own minds about which approach is being followed. A failure to do this often results in confused thinking and presentation and a serious imbalance in the programme as experienced by the pupils. The approach we adopt will therefore determine what we are trying to achieve through a particular topic.

Topic

The topic should be a brief heading designating the piece of content that is being used as the focus for exploration. The wording of this heading is particularly important since it defines a specific area for exploration. The basic criteria for the choice of topic should be that it is worthwhile in itself as an area of exploration, and that it has the best potential for achieving the objectives and furthering children's understanding. In the case of units of work following the systems approach, the choice of topics will be determined by these criteria, and by the nature of the tradition being studied. In other words, topics will be related to the kind of themes and areas that are important within that tradition. For example, beliefs about God and theistic spirituality will be explored while studying most religious traditions. However, these would be inappropriate topics when studying the Buddhist tradition, as they are not central to that system.

Content overview

The purpose of writing an overview is to give a succinct summary, in teacher language, of what the unit is all about in terms of its general aim, content or subject matter. Teachers can use this exercise to clarify in their own minds, and to convey clearly to other teachers, the basic intentions of the unit. The elements which might be included in this summary are:

- Where does this topic fit into the field of enquiry?

- Why is it being explored with children in this age range?
- How does this unit relate to previous and future units in advancing children's understanding?

Objectives

With the introduction of the National Curriculum, the term 'objectives' has largely been replaced by 'Statements of Attainment'. When we refer to objectives in this manual, we mean clearly written, unambiguous statements which are capable of translation into practical classroom activities. We are also referring to what might be assessed in RE.

Of course, the individual and local situation will determine whether teachers formulate their own objectives or whether they work with Statements of Attainment prescribed in their agreed syllabus or other locally determined document. In either case, however, all teachers need to formulate or select suitable statements which are specific to particular units of work (if not lessons) and are consistent with the aims of the subject. We have, therefore, adopted the following three categories of unit objectives which may guide the teacher in formulating his or her own statements and which also provide a framework for those who need to select from locally determined documents. The balance of these three broad objectives will vary from age group to age group. In some cases there will be more emphasis on acquiring and organising new knowledge; in others the prime concern will be to extend understanding, while at other times the clear intention will be to encourage pupils to reflect on the beliefs, values and attitudes being explored.

Knowing

Every RE unit of work seeks to communicate to pupils (or rather to help them to discover), an important body of knowledge which arises out of the subject's extensive and complex field of enquiry. This is material which the pupils can learn, and, at an appropriate time and in an appropriate manner, recall and express. Ideally each unit should help pupils assimilate new knowledge and/or reinforce previously acquired knowledge.

Understanding

These kinds of objectives focus on ideas and concepts and the complex relationship between them and isolated items of knowledge. They are concerned with promoting the pupil's appreciation of deeper meanings, and their understanding of the relative significance of difficult items of knowledge which they may glean about the subject under investigation.

Reflecting

At the heart of this subject is the human need to formulate or acquire a set of beliefs and values. The process by which individuals and groups acquire such beliefs and values is extremely complex. As already indicated it is not the role of RE in schools to prescribe what any individual's pattern of belief and behaviour will be. It is its task to help pupils to reflect, at a deeply personal level, on all the different beliefs and values, including their own, which are made available for exploration. Reflecting in this context means to evaluate in an honest and informed way, the worth and relevance of particular beliefs and values and the behaviour patterns which are likely to accompany them.

Activities

Here the word activities refers to all those things which teachers and pupils do in the context of a school lesson which further the objectives. Of course, many other things which teachers and pupils do in the course of any given lesson are not directly related to subject and lesson objectives. They may be of a management, pastoral or disciplinary kind. Whether they are planned, intentional, or spontaneous, they are all part and parcel of teaching.

However, at this planning level we are concerned with identifying a large number of activities which teachers can use in different ways and situations to achieve some or all of the three kinds of unit objectives described above.

At the unit stage of planning, it is probably best to include as wide a range as possible of potential activities so that the unit is not tied to any one year or group of children. Setting out activities for units of work is an exercise to help the teacher to think round some of the different ways in which the topic may be explored. The activities need not be in any order or have a logical connection between them. At a later stage, in the sequencing of activities for lessons, the teacher will need to select the most suitable ones and arrange them in a teachable sequence. A further advantage in setting out activities in this way at the stage of unit planning is that other teachers can make use of the suggestions, at the same time using their own judgement about selection and sequence.

When writing out these teaching/learning activities some of the following points may be borne in mind:

- Give a clear indication of the nature of the activity in the form of an instruction to the teacher.
- Indicate the kind of subject matter you intend to explore. Give examples.
- Suggest ways in which the classroom may be organised and arranged to promote interaction between children or to advance their understanding.

Clearly, all the activities need to reflect the needs, capabilities and comprehension levels of the children for whom the unit is intended. At this planning level it is also important to ensure that each activity is relatively self-contained and that there is more than one activity designed to achieve the same objective. This allows teachers to make choices in the light of their own circumstances.

By way of a brief checklist we offer here a summary of the kinds of activities which form the basic media through which pupils get access to and acquire some share of human knowledge, understanding and experience. Skilled teachers of RE will include all of these in their teaching repertoire.

acting	playing
dancing	reading
drawing	recording
filming	singing
listening	smelling
looking	talking
making	tasting
miming	writing
painting	

Resources

The teacher's task in the classroom may be described as 'prismatic' – it is to draw together and select from the great wealth of human experience a very limited number of examples and to focus attention on them sharply. The world 'out there' has to be brought into the classroom for children to explore. Teaching resources are the means through which this is done.

The structure of this manual throughout has been deductive, starting from principles and working down to practicalities. This is, of course, not the practical way in which many – maybe most – teachers work. The choice of resources is a case in point. Ideally, resources should be chosen in order to meet objectives, not vice versa. In practice, a 'good' resource becomes available and a teacher plans a unit of work around it. Clearly, there has to be a compromise, because the ideal resources are rarely available, and in any case there are no resource items which are absolutely indispensable to RE. The basic principle, however, in selecting resources is that they must further the objectives and genuinely contribute to learning.

Much of the subject matter of RE can only be made available in the classroom through the use of a variety of resources such as
- books (class sets or single copies for reference)
- charts and maps (normally for display)
- pictures and posters (large format for display, small for group work)
- audio-cassettes
- slides and filmstrips
- artefacts (including ritual objects, dress, food, etc.)
- video
- computer software

To these must be added a range of materials for writing, drawing and modelling, filming, etc.

Religious Education

School _____

Age range _____   **Approach** Systems/Life Themes _____

Topic _____

Objectives: Knowing   _____
_____
_____

Understanding   _____
_____
_____

Reflecting   _____
_____
_____

Activities   _____
_____
_____
_____
_____
_____
_____
_____
_____
_____
_____
_____
_____
_____
_____
_____
_____

Resources   _____
_____
_____
_____

Assessment   _____
_____
_____
_____

Figure 25   Plan for a unit of work

Ceremonies associated with infants

Approach: systems

Content overview

Pupils at this early stage of primary education will be familiar with important events in their own family life. Such things as birthdays and anniversaries are examples. However, they may not be familiar with specifically Christian ceremonies. As the unit does assume that pupils are aware of the ways in which families celebrate special events, they can be helped to understand these particular Christian ceremonies even if they have not yet seen one actually take place.

Christians of all denominations recognise the importance of nurturing their children in the Christian faith. Most Christians indicate this shortly after the birth of a child with a ceremony at their own church. Two main forms of ceremony are associated with infants. The first is infant baptism in which a child is accepted into the membership of the Christian Church. The use of water is the central symbol of this ceremony or sacrament. The second form of service is dedication and thanksgiving. Very few, if any, physical symbols are used by Christians who prefer this second form.

Parents, guardians and godparents may all take a direct part in these ceremonies and in many cases they will occur within the context of a congregational act of worship.

The focus of this unit is on the various practices associated with these ceremonies. Christian beliefs are of course implicit in these outward actions and in later years pupils will be helped to study them in a more direct way.

Aims

Knowing

1 the names of the various Christian ceremonies associated with infants, infant baptism, christening, chrismation, dedication and thanksgiving;
2 some details about the use of water, candles, oil, certificates and presents during these ceremonies;
3 the promises made by parents, guardians, godparents and the congregation.

Understanding that

1 the birth of babies can bring a lot of happiness;
2 many families show this happiness through special events;
3 some parents recognise that their baby belongs to others such as grandparents, brothers and sisters as well as themselves;
4 Christians have a special service in their church to show their belief that the baby also belongs to the Christian family and to God.

Reflecting on

1 the Christian belief that all people belong to God;
2 our own dependence on somebody.

Activities

The following activities are some examples of work which can be undertaken to achieve the aims of this particular unit across the lower primary age band. It is left to teachers' professional judgement to select, add to and sequence learning activities which suit their particular situations.

- Display pictures of infant baptism and thanksgiving and dedication services drawn from various Christian denominations. Ensure that a variety of different examples are available to the pupils. Encourage the pupils to talk about what they see. Talk about what is happening and how the people involved might be feeling. Explain as simply as possible what happens in at least two of the ceremonies.
- Visit one or more local churches which practise infant baptism. Explain to the pupils the location, the type and design of the font. In some churches it is near the door. In others it is in the centre or focus

of worship. Some churches use a very small font, others a large and ornate one. Ask the local priest/ minister to explain and perhaps read to the pupils some of the words from the baptism service, particularly the promises made by parents and godparents, and to answer the pupils' questions.

- Invite to the class a Christian family who have recently had their child baptised or dedicated. Let the pupils see the infant and ask the mother or father to tell the children about the service. If the family has a baptism candle or baptism certificate, show this to the pupils. Explain any unusual words or symbols.
- Show a video of an infant baptism. Encourage the pupils to talk about what they have seen. Let those who have been baptised or have attended a baptism talk to the rest of the class about it.
- Explain that names often have a special meaning. Give examples using a boy's and a girl's name. The use of the baby's own name is important in Christian ceremonies of baptism or dedication. Some Christian parents deliberately choose names of Bible characters or saints for their children, for example John, Mark, Ruth, Mary, Nicholas. Give the pupils cards containing the words 'My name is …', 'My name means …' and 'I have the same name as …'. Some of these may have to be taken home for parents to fill in. Discuss the results, including those from children of non-Christian back- grounds; draw attention to Christian names which are the same as those of notable Christians, past and present.
- Make a large display chart of several different types of baptismal fonts, for example a large free-standing font, a small table font, a large font for immersing the child. Help children through discussion to understand the different ways in which these are used. Stress the fact that in all cases water is used as a symbol of washing and refreshment.

- Show a picture depicting the baptism of Jesus by John the Baptist. Read one account of this from the New Testament (e.g. Matthew 3: 13–17). Explain to the children that Christians believe that Jesus is God's son and that this act of baptising with water is now very important to most of his followers. Read Jesus's last command to his followers (Matthew 18: 18–20) and draw attention to the command to baptise people. Explain that when Christians do this they are showing that they believe in and obey Jesus and that they want other people to follow Jesus.
- Tell or read the New Testament story about Jesus taking very small children on his knee and blessing them (Mark 10: 13–16). Allow time for children to react to the story and to any pictures depicting the event. Explain how many Christians tell this story to show their belief that God loves all people, including very young babies. When they baptise or dedicate little babies in church they are expressing this belief and welcoming the new baby into their Christian family.
- By using a large doll demonstrate ways in which Christians use water, oils, candles and certificates during baptismal or dedication ceremonies. Perhaps some water and oil could be sprinkled or poured on to pupils' heads so that they can experience how it feels. Encourage children to talk freely about what they have seen and felt.

Resources
- artefacts: baptismal candles, cards, certificate, portable font
- large pictures showing baptisms, for example Stages of Life 4 and Natural World 9 from *Life Themes in the Early Years*, Westhill Project
- *Christians 1* – Westhill Project

Figure 26   Planning a unit of work for the infant school

Attitudes to poverty

Approach: life themes

Content overview

Poverty is one of the key issues in shared human experience through which ultimate questions about dignity and value can be raised most clearly. It is an area of the greatest relevance to young people growing up in the modern world.

By this stage, adolescents should be able to build on knowledge and understanding of this issue gained earlier in RE and in other subject areas, and on their awareness derived from the media.

There should not therefore be much need to go into detail on the causes of poverty or to examine particular situations or some of the political and economic solutions, except where they raise ultimate questions and moral issues. The focus of the unit is clearly on attitudes. There does need to be an awareness of the distinction between absolute and relative poverty, and between enforced and voluntary poverty. The unit will emphasise an understanding of the issues and help to raise questions in the students' minds about people's responses – including their own. This unit will form part of a series of units which explores issues and beliefs.

Objectives

Knowing

1 the difference between absolute and relative poverty
2 the difference between enforced and voluntary poverty
3 several examples of attitudes towards poverty.

Understanding

1 some of the beliefs that underlie the attitudes
2 some of the moral questions that are raised by these attitudes.

Reflecting on

1 what it means to be poor
2 the belief that we all share responsibility for each other/belong to each other
3 our own attitudes to poverty.

Activities

The following activities are some examples of work which can be undertaken to achieve the aims of this particular unit across the upper secondary age band. It is left to teachers' professional judgement to select, add to and sequence learning activities which suit their particular situation.

- Have the students make two lists, one setting out what they think are essential needs and the other setting out what they think are luxuries.
- Get them to compare these lists in groups. Try to arrive at a consensus of five basic needs.
- Have each student prepare a questionnaire to put to their peers/staff/relatives on their attitudes to poverty.
- Remind students, briefly, of some of the factors which contribute to poverty, e.g. climate, sanitation, conflict, corruption.
- Show an audiovisual programme which illustrates differing religious attitudes to, and beliefs about, the causes and cures of poverty, for example Girl in Brazil (BBC Scene).
- Distribute information about Christian Aid, for example 'Why Christian Aid?' and 'Christian Aid today'.
- Pupils working in small groups identify and list some of the key beliefs about poverty expressed in these documents.
- Have the students carry out some research into Muslim teaching about zakat and attitudes to wealth and poverty.
- Set up a debate on the motion that 'Earth has enough for every man's need but not every man's greed (Gandhi)'.
- Invite a Christian nun to speak to the class about her vow of poverty.

Resources

- Wall chart showing some basic causes of poverty
- CAFOD project pack 'People in Brazil'
- BBC Scene series (BBC Television for schools) – Girl in Brazil
- Christian Aid information packs
- *Christians 4* and Christians Photopack – Westhill Project.

Figure 27 Planning a unit of work for the upper secondary school

Along with these inanimate resources, teachers of RE have an even more important, though understandably less used, set of human resources. Our earlier discussion on the field of enquiry stressed the important role of teachers' and children's own individual patterns of belief and behaviour as a potential source of content. Although these are always present in the classroom it is not always appropriate and easy to make them explicit and thus use them as subject matter for a particular lesson. Another obvious and highly valuable human resource may be found among other members of staff and members of local communities.

Again, important though these are, practical considerations and the inability of many people to articulate their beliefs and experiences in front of children make it difficult to use this pool of local resources. Nevertheless, an awareness of the difficulties should not prevent the imaginative and keen teacher from using such people sparingly and with sensitivity. When they are used, either in the classroom or at a place away from the school, it is important that teachers retain the management initiative and control. The visitor, as visitor, is a resource and not a replacement teacher. It is the teacher's professional responsibility to ensure that appropriate learning is taking place in accordance with the unit objectives.

Reference to resources at this stage of planning units should be specific. Where necessary there should be some indication of which resource item is recommended for use with particular activities.

2 Preparing lessons from units of work

Preparing lessons is, of course, a basic and continual task for teachers. As this is a manual intended primarily to help practising professional teachers improve their performance in relation to RE, an understanding of the basic skills of teaching is taken for granted.

It may be helpful, however, for even the most experienced teacher to reflect again on some essential elements of the task of preparing RE lessons in the light of the contemporary nature of the subject. The following are worthy of consideration.

Lesson segments

Traditionally the shape of an RE lesson has been the presentation of material by the teacher followed by some form of pupil expression work, note-taking and discussion. The emphasis was on teacher input with a minimal amount of pupil participation in the discovery or generation of significant amounts of the content of the lesson.

In stressing the inclusion of activities when designing units, we have pointed to an additional, if not alternative, shape. The lesson can be planned as a series of segments or activities which focus on a central topic and contribute in different ways to the achievement of the unit aims.

While in most cases each segment will have a natural and logical relationship with both the one that precedes it and the one that follows, this will not always be the case. On some occasions there can be within the one lesson an abrupt and complete change in style – for example, some unexpected happening in the classroom or elsewhere which the teacher is able to use to better advantage than continuing with the planned activity. Such abrupt changes can also be planned to show that the topic can be explored in different ways and from quite different perspectives. Deeper levels of understanding and reflection often result from such changes in activity styles.

The number of segments and the length of each segment within any given lesson will be determined by many factors. More important among them are the time available, the extent of the pupils' attention spans and the nature of the activity itself. For example, a finger painting segment with infant children may take more time than the telling of a story to the same group; a brainstorm session in an upper secondary class round the problems of violence will be much shorter than a formal debate about the value of pacifist beliefs or stances within different world religions.

Sequencing segments in a lesson

There is seldom any one right order in which to arrange the segments of a lesson once they have been selected. Here again teachers have to use their own professional judgement in the light of their immediate circumstances and their perception of the needs, interests and abilities of the pupils.

Alongside considerations of time and the logic of the subject matter, teachers should also take account of other roles that different activities can play in promoting and furthering the learning process. Depending very largely on where it comes in a lesson, an activity may be used to open up a topic, to encourage pupil participation and feedback, to develop understanding and to reinforce what has been covered previously.

The need to motivate

As all teachers know only too well, every child entering the classroom is not necessarily ready or willing to engage in the learning planned. The art of good teaching certainly includes the ability to capture the attention of at least the majority of the class and then to focus that attention on the subject at hand.

Activities designed to achieve this motivating purpose clearly come at the beginning of a lesson. There will be occasions however when some kind of attention-restoring activity is necessary at other points in the lesson. This is especially so with very young children and in lessons which occupy a rather long period of time.

In the context of RE it is also worth remembering that a great deal of the subject's content is interesting and may be already important to children. Providing them with a ready access to more information and with clear guidelines as to how they might explore the subject further, and express their responses to it, can often be highly motivating. The teacher does not always have to resort to gimmicky, amusing or disciplinary techniques in order to capture and retain pupils' attention.

The need to explore

A great deal has been said throughout this manual about the extensiveness and complexity of the RE field of enquiry. With such an enormous amount of interesting and challenging material to explore, it is surprising to discover that many pupils often describe its treatment in schools as boring, repetitive and irrelevant. Not all the blame for this can be laid at the teacher's door. Many very powerful influences are at work in the pupils' homes, among their peers and in society generally to reinforce such attitudes; but there is also evidence that when pupils are helped in imaginative ways to explore the mysteries, questions, beliefs, experiences and practices associated with religions in an open, informed and non-dogmatic way, they are capable of sustained intellectual enquiry and emotional involvement.

To achieve this, teachers need to select activities which provide pupils with opportunities to expand their knowledge and deepen their understanding of the subject's total field of enquiry. There is no excuse for an RE programme in schools which pupils can honestly describe as repeating the same old things year after year. No one using this manual will have reached this point without getting the clear message that the subject can be planned in a developmental way so that pupils know that they are exploring new material in increasingly demanding ways.

Teachers can be well satisfied if a significant number of their pupils leave their classes making such comments as, 'I never knew that before' or 'That is the first time that I have really understood what X is all about'. As pointed out above, this kind of response is in itself motivation for further exploration and discovery. One lesson's exploration activities may well provide another lesson with its motivation segment.

The need to express

A great deal has been said so far about the nature of contemporary RE and the ways in which it can be approached and structured to achieve its general aim. This in turn demands of teachers that they provide ample scope for pupils to express, through a variety of media, their own beliefs and values and the relationship which these may have to those traditional belief systems being explored in the RE programme.

If, as we have claimed, the aim of RE is to help pupils mature in relation to their own individual pattern of belief, then an increasing ability to identify and articulate how and why they differ from alternative commitments would seem to be an essential skill to be acquired. The aims and objectives of the subject require lesson activities which provide opportunities for pupil expression.

Implicit in such an aim is a further claim that the pupil's present pattern of belief, however immature, confused or ill-informed, is a potential source of content. This potential content can only become available for exploration and evaluation if and when it is given coherent expression in the classroom. While teachers cannot plan in advance to use such content on any given occasion, they can design activities which provide maximum opportunity and freedom for pupils to give expression to their own ideas and their responses to the range of beliefs being explored.

Anyone familiar with the major world religions will know that deeply held beliefs and convictions are not adequately expressed simply in descriptive prose or through the language and concepts of historical or scientific investigation and discourse. The whole range of expressive and imaginative forms of communication is used and RE, if it is to be true to its subject matter and aims, must advance pupils' skills in relation to their use. Just as the belief systems have, since they began, expressed themselves through art, music, story, poetry, ritual, symbol and drama, so must RE lessons provide pupils with regular opportunities to express their beliefs and ideas through these different media.

If a further case for the inclusion of expressive activities in RE were needed, it is surely to be found in the important teaching task of pupil assessment and feedback. The effectiveness of each of the types of assessment (diagnostic, formative and summative) is almost entirely dependent on the pupils' ability to express themselves clearly and with increasing sophistication. (See Part Five.)

To reiterate, there is no one set pattern or sequence of activities for all RE lessons. Teachers will find their own style for planning lessons which, on most occasions combine segments which motivate pupils and help them to explore and express faith responses.

3 Organisation in the classroom

Here we are concerned mainly with the range of different groupings of pupils which seem possible, desirable and practical when preparing and presenting RE lessons. An understanding of these ought to contribute to a more efficient management of the programme, whether it takes place in a traditional or multiple area type of school, and whether it is a primary, middle or secondary school. A willingness and ability to use a variety of physical arrangements in the classroom can provide scope for a greater range of teaching activities and therefore learning experiences for pupils.

The following symbols illustrate the variety of organisation methods and a selection of their combined uses.

A large group

In this case the class or year group is kept in one large group and all pupils attend to the same activity. This will usually be in the form of direct teacher input, e.g. lecturing, telling, demonstrating, story-telling, questioning or audiovisual presentation.

Medium-sized groups

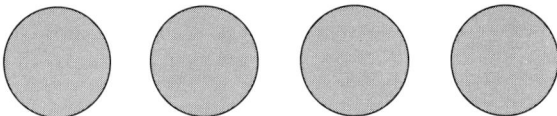

Pupils are arranged in a number of medium-sized groups, with perhaps five to ten pupils in a group. Some may be directly taught, especially if a team-teaching situation exists; others may be engaged in some form of self-directed work, e.g. discussion, research, project work or planning.

Small groups

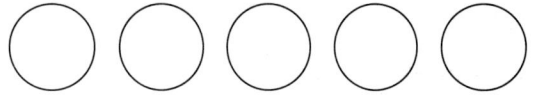

On these occasions two to five pupils are working together, usually on a specific task set by the teacher or selected from a series of electives. This can be a useful management device in mixed ability classes, provided that there are sufficient resources available to support the range of activities prepared.

Individual work

The emphasis here is more on how the pupils are working rather than on any physical arrangement. Provided that conditions are conducive to the kind of activity and work expected, the actual classroom arrangements are less significant.

Teacher/pupil interaction

A triangle with its apex above the base line can be used to show when the teacher is directly addressing the group.

A triangle pointing downwards indicates a situation where pupils report back on their work or direct questions to the teacher and/or the whole class.

Teaching and learning patterns

Clearly these components can be arranged in very many different ways. Part of the teacher's task in planning to capture and maintain pupils' interest lies in varying the pattern so that the situation is not too often repeated, or so that pupils are not required to spend too long in any one situation.

By combining these symbols we may present diagrammatically a number of possible patterns of pupil arrangement, which teachers can use and thus again expand their teaching repertoire.

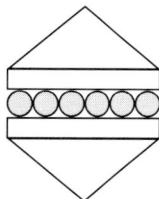

This is a fairly standard pattern. The teacher introduces the topic to the whole class, who then divide into medium-sized groups for discussion. Towards the end of the time, the groups report back to the whole of the class.

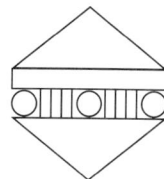

This is another familiar pattern. After the general introduction, pupils, either individually or in small groups, get on with their work. Feedback is directly to the teacher(s) and not to the whole class.

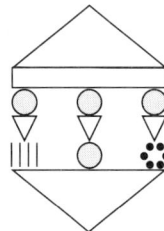

This is a slightly more complex structure possibly requiring a longer period of time. After the introduction, pupils are set in three medium-sized groups. These report progress to the teacher who then sets further work, either for individuals, the larger group, or small groups. Final reporting or presentation is to the whole class.

4 Presenting religious matters in the classroom

The concern here is not about the nature and function of so-called 'religious language'. It is to do with ways of talking about and presenting religious matters in an open educational context.

Most experienced teachers are well aware of the need to use words that are meaningful to pupils. For example it is not helpful to use technical religious terms unless their meaning is explained, or to use terms which are beyond the present experience or comprehension level of the pupils. Similarly, difficulties in communication arise when terms which have multiple meanings or have a range of associations are used without detailed explanation. Words like 'meek' and 'father', important within the Christian tradition, may be understood in very different ways depending on their accepted usage among people with whom pupils live and perhaps on the experiences that pupils have had. Terms which produce positive feelings in some people may have negative meanings for others.

However there are a few other language styles and conventions which are required of teachers when they are presenting religious matters within the context of RE. A failure to adopt and maintain these conventions often results in both a breakdown in communication and in increasing resentment on the part of many pupils.

While these conventions are essential to the purposes of RE, they are not unique to it. They are in fact used by most adults when they engage in conversation with others about controversial issues. These are accepted protocols and manners which are used to avoid any appearance of pushing one's own ideas and beliefs 'down someone else's throat'. Adults exercising these protocols endeavour to show respect for each other's views while at the same time taking the opportunity to voice, strongly if need be, personally held convictions.

In order to make clear the nature of these conventions and to stress their importance for RE, we introduce the notion of 'owning and grounding'.

Owning and grounding

Central to this need to own or ground belief statements is the distinction between 'fact' and 'belief' types of statement. Among other things, such statements are those about which differences of outlook are found within the community. Particularly in RE, they include statements about God, claims about religious leaders or interpretations of sacred books. For example, in speaking about Jesus, a distinction may be made between saying that he lived at a particular time in a particular place and that he was the Christ who died for the sins of the whole world in accordance with God's plan. The first statement could be the factual reporting of any observer and is potentially open to historical research. The latter statement presumes a belief about who Jesus was and thus is of a different kind.

It is possible, indeed it is essential to the purposes of RE, that both kinds of statements be used in the classroom and that pupils become aware of the distinction between them and skilled in using them appropriately.

Sometimes teachers and pupils may own a particular belief as theirs, by the use of such terms as 'I believe ...', 'It seems to me that ...', 'I feel ...', 'I think ...', or 'In my experience ...'.

Alternatively they may ground the belief by attaching it to some groups of people who hold it, or to some source from which it comes, for example, 'Muslims believe ...', or 'It says in the Qur'an ...', or 'Some/many people do not believe ...'.

Owning or grounding a belief does not prove or assume that it is true or authoritative for others. However, because it does not presume upon their agreement the pupils are more likely to be able to hear and to discuss what is being presented and may not feel that particular beliefs or values are being forced on them.

When beliefs are owned or grounded they sound less dogmatic, and some may fear they will sound less authoritative. However, when the source of their authority, whether in personal experience or in a tradition, is made clear, this provides important data for those who are being asked to consider where they stand in relation to those beliefs. A quick way to check the authority or source of a belief statement is to ask 'Who says it?' or 'Who believes it?' This assists teachers and/or pupils either to own the statement or to ground it by indicating who believes it to be true.

Several benefits can be seen to follow when belief statements are either owned or grounded:

1 Teachers have greater freedom to deal with their own beliefs in class.
2 Conversation about beliefs becomes more open and easier to develop, in that once teachers and pupils learn either to own or to ground statements of belief, it is easier for others to respond with their beliefs, whether these are the same or different.
3 By this approach teachers do not presume upon the beliefs of their pupils, so helping to avoid the negative reactions and discipline problems that such presumption can generate.
4 Most religions acknowledge the importance of faith decisions as part of the development of religious maturity. However, when beliefs are referred to as if everyone thinks that way, the role of decision is hidden. In contrast, if beliefs are owned or grounded the issue is brought into the open for consideration. In this way pupils can become aware of the importance of these decisions, without any implication of an attempt to enforce or require commitment to a particular belief.
5 Some pupils are placed in a situation of

tension when they receive contradictory views on belief issues from various significant adults. The language of teachers can heighten this tension or it can support and encourage the pupils in working out their own patterns of belief. If these conventions of owning and grounding are maintained from the earliest primary school years, pupils may be better prepared to work through the faith struggles which often characterise the teenage years.
6 One of the difficulties facing teachers of RE is that of making the content as concrete as possible. When beliefs are owned or grounded they are linked to individuals or groups who hold them. This will help to make them more concrete in that the beliefs are seen as having implications for people's lives.
7 When referring to sacred writings, care in owning and grounding can help clarify the way in which they are being used. This will involve distinguishing between (i) quotations (ii) interpretations or summary statements based on someone's reading of the text and (iii) implicit claims concerning the authority of the book in people's lives. For example, the statement 'The Guru Granth Sahib says ...' is a form of grounding if it can be followed by the question 'Where does it say it?'
8 Owning or grounding their references to beliefs can help teachers communicate more easily. It enables them to speak in a way that is inclusive of all pupils, without making assumptions about prior commitments. It also provides an example which can assist the pupils in giving clearer expression to their own beliefs and attitudes.

PART FIVE

How can RE be assessed?

The basic premise of this Part is that assessment of the work of children is as important in Religious Education as in any other area of the curriculum. Since we are dealing with a subject which claims the same basis in education as any other subject, we need to follow the same educational principles. One of these is that assessment is an essential part of the learning process. Without some form of assessment we cannot discover the level of understanding which children already have, whether children are making progress or what they may have learned as a result of our teaching. Moreover, the point that will be stressed in this Part is that assessment is itself one of the means by which children learn.

There have been in the past, and still are in many schools, a number of serious difficulties which impede the carrying out of useful assessment in this subject. Some of these difficulties arise from uncertainty in the minds of some teachers about what we are actually assessing in RE. We are assessing the development of children's understanding about religion and their own personal response to it. In other words we are assessing the extent to which pupils gradually increase their knowledge and understanding of what this manual calls the RE field of enquiry. We are also assessing pupils' willingness and ability to reflect on the issues, questions and experiences which emerge from it.

There are, however, some obvious difficulties in assessing, in any formal way, the early development of understanding in very young children in the primary school. The emphasis here will be on those more informal and intuitive assessments which teachers of young primary children are making all the time. Discussions with individual children, listening to their conversations and encouraging their self expression, will all provide pointers to the children's development in this area of the curriculum. Since it will not be either possible or desirable to draw distinctive subject boundaries in the work they are doing, the assessments will obviously be more wide-ranging than those simply limited to an assessment of children's understanding of religion. Nonetheless, whether formal or informal, assessment will be an integral part of children's learning and of the teacher's awareness of progress and development.

Other difficulties arise from practical considerations, particularly those of the timetable in the secondary school. Where one teacher is asked to teach a subject to virtually every child for one thirty-five minute period each week, it is almost impossible to carry out any meaningful assessment of the progress of individual children. Meaningful assessment can only be carried out where there is appropriate provision on the timetable for the teaching of the subject.

The exercise of assessment depends entirely on the goals or objectives that a teacher sets out to achieve. Assessment is therefore concerned with measuring the extent to which those objectives have been achieved. Objectives can be set at various levels, ranging from the total school programme down to individual lessons. They require the most careful thought to ensure that they are realistic, attainable and, as far as possible, assessable. This manual does not deal in detail with objectives at every level, but examples of unit objectives are given as illustrations in Part Four.

1 Purposes of assessment

Before examining these in detail, it is important to include here a few general points regarding assessment and its role in the teaching and learning process:

- Assessment is part of the process of teaching and learning, and needs to be built into the planning of RE.
- The word 'assessment' is derived from the Latin 'assidere' meaning 'to sit down beside'.
- It involves informed judgements about pupils' achievements and progress.
- It is intended to draw attention to pupils' positive achievements.
- Assessment can take place on any occasion when pupils express themselves, intentionally or otherwise, in relation to learning objectives.
- It is based on evidence of what pupils know, understand and can do.
- Assessment is usually made by the teacher, but may include judgements made by the pupils themselves.
- It implies a contract of trust between teachers and pupils. Both parties recognise, accept and value this partnership as a means of making progress.

With this overview in mind, we can now look at the different types of assessment and the purpose of each. Broadly speaking these may be divided into three areas:

1 *Diagnostic*: Finding out the level of understanding children have at the beginning of a course.
2 *Formative*: Helping to reinforce what they are learning.
3 *Summative*: Finding out what they have learned at the end of a course and, where necessary, putting them into grades.

Diagnostic

At the beginning of any long course of work – such as the start of a year, or the move from primary to secondary school, or where a new teacher takes over – it is important to know where the children are starting from, and what level of knowledge and understanding they bring to the course. This is particularly pertinent at the start of secondary schooling, where children normally come from a range of feeder primary schools in which the level of development of religious understanding may be varied.

Diagnostic assessment is necessarily broad. It will range over wide areas and cover as much ground as possible. It is not really concerned with specific details, but with general knowledge and understanding. If a first-year secondary teacher is proposing to start the year by looking at some general questions about religion, the teacher will want to know something about the understanding that the children already have. There is no need to explore the wealth of detailed information that the children may or may not have acquired, though there are some very basic items of factual knowledge about religion that children ought to know before they leave the primary school.

It is also necessary for the secondary teacher to bear in mind that the appearance of the RE dimension in the primary school may be quite different from that which dominates in the secondary school; for example, children may have no real perception of RE as a separate subject. Thus the forms of diagnostic testing used must reflect an integrated approach and allow each child to draw on examples from a variety of different religions, since it is unlikely that they will have covered precisely the same traditions in exactly the same way.

Any diagnostic test will, therefore, need to explore children's general awareness and understanding with great flexibility in regard to the use of the particular examples used.

Using questions as a diagnostic basis

Set out below is a range of general areas of understanding which teachers in lower secondary classes will need to assess before they can plan appropriate programmes of RE for pupils entering their schools. Of course, the closer the liaison between secondary schools and their feeder primary schools, the easier it is to ensure that the curricula in both schools are designed to achieve this kind of progressive learning in regard to RE.

- Are pupils aware of diversity in religious belief and practice?
- Are they willing to explore the beliefs and practices of others in an open way?
- Do they have more than a formal knowledge of facts about religions?
- In particular, have they begun to explore the 'hidden' elements of belief, value and spirituality?

- Are they able to discern the way in which language is used by religions in a metaphorical and parabolic way?
- Do they have an understanding of what symbols and myths are for?
- Are they able to recognise a moral issue?
- Are they able to recognise an ultimate question?
- Are they able to hold a discussion on a controversial issue in a tolerant and frank way?
- Do they have anything more than a formal understanding of concepts such as 'God' or 'faith'?

Formative

For the purposes of RE this is the most important element in assessment. It is designed to help children in the learning process and to assist them towards mastering an understanding of the subject. Regular assessment (by a variety of techniques) is one of the ways of reinforcing learning. When children have explored a particular topic, their understanding of it and the knowledge they have gained can actually be strengthened and deepened by this form of assessment. It also provides a guideline for the teacher who wants to know how much progress children have made in meeting the set objectives. Formative assessment is related to short units of work and takes place at frequent intervals.

Formative assessment is concerned with very specific objectives over a relatively short period of time. It will therefore be used to assess matters of detail related to a specific unit of work. It should elicit evidence about how far children have taken in the information they have been dealing with, and how far they have understood it. At the same time, the teacher will use this opportunity also to observe how far children are continuing to use some of the basic principles of the subject they have already learned. For example, in a class discussion are they able to wait their turn or to disagree without shouting, or, in an exercise in picture analysis, do they show imagination in the questions they ask?

Since we are concerned here with using assessment actually to reinforce learning, it follows that this aim will only be achieved if children are given the maximum opportunity to learn from the assessment. This means that feedback is essential. The feedback, however, is not for comparative or competitive purposes ('How many have I got right?') but to further the learning process. In other words, it should help the child to identify errors or false assumptions and to ask questions about them in order to clarify them. It can also help the teacher to make decisions about whether to go over a piece of work again, or whether to introduce more detailed and varied examples to illustrate a concept – or whether the exploration can be taken to a deeper level because the children have quickly grasped the issues.

Summative

This term is used to describe assessment procedures which take place at the end of a course of work. It can apply to such formal assessments as end-of-year examinations and particularly to external examinations such as GCSE. Recent thinking, however, has tended, rightly, to place less emphasis on the value of this form of assessment and more on the regular, on-going assessment carried out by teachers over a period of time in order to build up a more rounded picture of a pupil's progress. Terminal tests, where they are used, can only provide a limited confirmation of the conclusions drawn from formative assessments by teachers.

2 Some guiding principles in assessing RE

Assessing RE has to be related to the main areas of achievement with which the subject deals. This means that we are looking for developing and progressive achievement in the following areas:

1 Ways of understanding the ideas, beliefs, values, attitudes and behaviour of others. This includes the ability to enter imaginatively into their experiences.
2 Awareness of some of the experiences of life which prompt questions about its meaning, value and purpose, and sensitivity to religious responses to these experiences and questions.
3 Developing their own values, beliefs and attitudes by reflecting on the experiences of others, and by responding to them in thoughtful and constructive ways.

As we have stressed in this manual, each of these elements of RE should have equal value. These will be inseparable from each other in the process of RE, so that any activity in Religious Education will help pupils to achieve something in all three elements.

Assessment will need to be related to a limited number of broad Statements of Attainment or objectives appropriate to each Key Stage. As a result of developments arising from the 1988 Education Reform Act, these statements will normally be set out in local authority documents. Each of these statements or objectives will

- represent an on-going process in a Key Stage, not a fixed point of achievement.
- be 'visited' on several occasions in different contexts in the course of that Key Stage.

- indicate an attainment which different pupils in a particular Key Stage may achieve at a variety of levels.
- require a variety of evidence and examples of achievement before broad conclusions can be drawn about how far pupils have progressed.

This means that teachers cannot simply test pupils on one occasion and conclude from the results that they have arrived at a fixed target. Assessments will be carried out on a number of occasions and in different contexts in order to gather evidence of achievement. The evidence will show that some pupils will grasp concepts or respond creatively better than others. Thus teachers will be able to differentiate levels of achievement in what pupils understand or can do. Once again, a note of caution is necessary. Whilst it is quite clear that there will be different levels of achievement in Key Stage One, it may be misleading to make such distinctions in an area of the curriculum like RE. On the other hand, because pupils may be more articulate and teachers may be able to make more detailed assessments in Key Stage Four, it is probably much more appropriate to differentiate levels of achievement by this stage.

The overriding principle is that ideas about possible achievements and outcomes need to be built into the planning of RE topics and units so that assessment is seen as an integral part of the learning process and not simply an unrelated afterthought.

3 Techniques of assessment in RE

Once we are reasonably clear about our objectives and the kind of evidence of achievement we are looking for, we need some ideas about how we can actually look for that evidence. This leads us into the area of techniques of assessment and the devising of assessment tasks.

The following are some broad principles that may guide our practice in this regard:

1 Assessment can take place at any time. Whenever pupils express themselves in any way in relation to stated objectives, there is an opportunity for making judgements and gathering evidence. These opportunities will often be found during activities which have not been specifically planned for assessment purposes.
2 Techniques and tasks should be as varied as possible to ensure that pupils can express themselves in different situations and in different ways.
3 Techniques and tasks need to be carefully related to the kind of learning experiences the pupils have had. This is the main reason why the assessment must be included in the planning of activities.
4 Assessment tasks should be either an ongoing development of what pupils are already doing or a task in which pupils can apply knowledge and understanding already gained to a new and unfamiliar situation.
5 Techniques and tasks of assessment have to be placed in the context of classroom management. The most varied and successful techniques and tasks are built upon very careful planning and control of the classroom situation.

The techniques and tasks we use in RE are meant to help teachers and pupils assess progress in relation to intended outcomes in the broad areas of knowledge, understanding and awareness, and personal thoughtful response that are central to RE.

For the reasons already given, we see very little value in using techniques which simply assess knowledge as 'remembered facts'. There is of course a place for testing memory by recall, but the main value of this lies in reinforcing learning. It is not in itself a basis for assessing understanding. Of much greater value is the assessment of understanding – not recalled understanding in the sense of simply being asked to remember an interpretation or application which has been taught. What we are concerned with is whether pupils can use and apply what they have been taught and what they have found out for themselves to a new situation or an unfamiliar context. Techniques and tasks need to be geared to eliciting how far pupils have developed this kind of understanding. Likewise, the responsive element of RE will be addressed through techniques and tasks which actually give pupils opportunities to express their own ideas.

Assessment opportunities

In the following examples from Key Stages One and Four, assessment and gathering evidence of achievement could take place during any of the activities shown in italics, as well as in formal assessment tasks. The emphasis is on the role of the teacher as observer and commentator, rather than detached tester.

At Key Stage One (lower primary)

The teacher has involved pupils in a number of different activities over a period of time, culminating in a visit to a local place of worship. The pupils *have been involved in play activities related to 'special events marking important occasions in people's lives', and they have participated in particular celebrations in class.* During the visit the teacher has given them plenty of opportunity to feel the atmosphere of the place and has stimulated their curiosity by asking them questions. They have met the leader of the community and have been shown some of the activities that take place to mark the special occasions.

During group activities in the classroom afterwards *the teacher engages them in discussion* about such questions as 'what do you think made this place different from our homes or from school?' and 'how did you feel about the place?' and 'what do you think it would be like if you took part in that special occasion?'. This sort of discussion is a natural progression from the activities that have already taken place.

The teacher uses the technique of observation and moves around the groups. Each group is engaged in different activities (art/craft, writing, perhaps listening to music) which are related to the questions. *The teacher spends some time with each group listening to their comments* in an informal way and encouraging the discussion with comments and questions.

What the teacher will be observing is 'talk'. In this case, however, he or she is not simply looking for evidence that they were stimulated by their experience, but that they are thinking about how a place of worship makes an occasion special.

The teacher would also be *observing and commenting on some of their other work which might supplement the evidence she has gathered from the pupils' talk.* As a follow-up to this activity the teacher might encourage some of the pupils *to present a short enactment* of a ceremony in which they imagine that they are in a place of worship. This might reinforce some of the comments already made to the pupils.

By using this kind of process the teacher has created a situation in the classroom in which he or she can assess the pupils by observing their reactions and responses.

At Key Stage Four (upper secondary)

In a unit of work on the problem of suffering, pupils are taking part in a self-directed task. *They start by working in groups*, identifying ways in which people suffer and trying to distinguish between those whose causes they think they can explain and those which seem to be beyond explanation. The teacher then shows a series of slides/pictures (without comment but possibly accompanied by appropriate music) to encourage their thoughtful reflection and develop their imagination. *Pupils then use a variety of sources* to consider some of the explanations of the problem of suffering, including non-religious explanations. These might include such stories as Job, Kisagotami and the Buddha, Jesus in the Garden of Gethsemane. Using the information they have gathered, pupils then begin to *collect material* of their own *in order to Prepare an individual presentation* in which they look at the question 'Why should this happen to me?' from the perspective of three different people in different situations. *They may present this* using a variety of media. The teacher might wish eventually to use two or three of these presentations with the whole class in order to illustrate different approaches. The teacher will comment on the pupils' work, particularly indicating ways in which the ideas in the presentation could be developed and carried forward.

In the context of GCSE, such a piece of work carried out and assessed in this way can provide an example of suitable course work for inclusion in the final assessment. The pupils will need to be clear about the objectives they are working to and understand the basis on which the work is being assessed. The teacher will need to give careful feedback to the pupils so that they can reflect on what they have achieved and note those points where they can improve.

Pupils' own perceptions of their achievements

It has become current practice in many schools to involve pupils in the assessment of their own progress through a system of profiling. This technique of assessment is a useful and informative addition to other assessments, both formal and informal, carried out by the teacher.

4 Recording and reporting RE

These two processes are essentially to do with

1 Selecting certain pieces of evidence from a great variety of possible evidence over a period of time.
2 Drawing conclusions from this evidence in order to report progress to parents.

The way these processes are carried out will be determined largely by school and LEA policy. However, for the purposes of RE, the procedures need to be

- simple and straightforward.
- based on the broad areas of achievement in the subject (Attainment Targets).
- open to pupils and parents.
- focused on positive achievements.

Recording RE

Our suggestion is that there should be four elements to recording RE:

- observation notes
- outcomes of tasks
- pupil profiles
- portfolio.

A simple record form could be used to keep information under these headings. To these might be added a summary report, a record of which the teacher retains to pass forward to the next year where necessary.

Observation notes

The first category for recording evidence consists of the notes a teacher may make of observations of pupil achievements. These may be gleaned from a number of situations in the classroom. For example, a teacher may have a discussion with a particular pupil; or may listen to a discussion between a group of pupils; or may observe the way an individual is working within a group.

The point behind these notes is that much of the evidence that is likely to be gathered from pupils about their progress in RE will come from this source. Pupils rarely show insight, awareness and sensitivity to order, but they do often show these qualities in unguarded moments and in informal situations. To miss this evidence and to confine ourselves to what pupils may do in set assessment situations or tasks would be to ignore a major indicator of how pupils are progressing.

We would want to stress that the gathering of observed evidence of this kind will apply in all Key Stages. Nevertheless, there will be a change of emphasis as pupils develop. We think that this process of recording observations will be the main source of evidence in Key Stage One. A report form would therefore need to be adapted to allow greater scope for this kind of comment. In Key Stage Four, however, greater emphasis may be placed on assessment tasks and the teacher's informal observations may be used to corroborate the evidence gathered from these tasks, especially where pupils find a formal assessment situation a difficult context in which to express themselves fully.

Observation notes do not need to be copious, and making and keeping these should not over-burden the teacher. Teachers will be highly selective in the notes they make. For example, the notes will be related to the three broad areas of content as outlined in Part 2. In a topic or theme where particular Statements of Attainment or objectives are being addressed, pupils may produce evidence of other, unintended attainments. These could be noted. A teacher might note an occasion where a pupil shows some clear insight or grasp of a particular understanding (for example, an understanding of another person's viewpoint) or a pupil might show evidence of a new level of awareness (for example, where they start to move towards a more sophisticated grasp of a key concept, or begin to interpret what they observe in non-literal ways). They may, on occasions, show a quite unusual or unexpected reaction which, while surprising, is nonetheless entirely valid. All these are valid points which a teacher could note. At the same time a teacher might need to note those aspects of a pupil's development which are causing real difficulty (for example, where some pupils find it hard to put some of their own ideas into words). The notes in this case provide a basis for some kind of remedial action.

Outcomes of tasks

A second element in the recording process involves situations where particular tasks are devised for assessment purposes. The outcomes of the tasks should be recorded in as simple a way as possible. There should be a developing degree of differentiation as pupils progress through school. Thus in Key Stage One, we should not try to differentiate, concentrating more on evidence drawn from observation, but in Key Stage Four we could differentiate broadly across four levels of achievement. There could be various devices for recording these outcomes from tasks. The traditional way is to use numerical marks. Another way is to use a simple form of coding. The teacher could put a line through or colour in a box to indicate the appropriate level of achievement. Thus for Key Stage Four, there could be a four-level pattern. Over a period of a year, it should be possible for a teacher to see, in broad terms, from the outcome of assessment tasks, how a pupil is making progress and what their overall level of achievement is.

Pupil profiles

These profiles, discussed earlier, can contribute to the overall picture of evidence. Thus they are both part of the process of learning and monitoring progress in which the pupils participate and they provide an on-going record. The teacher needs to record only that the profile relating to the topic has been completed. The teacher might also use the profiles for reporting purposes, a strategy which is discussed below. In this case, a note would need to be kept that the profile had been returned to school for later reference.

Portfolio

It has now become part of good practice for teachers to identify particular pieces of work done by pupils to be retained as evidence of progress. These could be pieces of work which reflect some of the points made above about teacher observations. Once again, careful selection by both teacher and pupil is important. Only a very limited number of pieces need to be identified for this purpose. By agreement with the pupil a simple strategy can be devised, such as using red stickers by which these pieces of work are identified. They are retained carefully so that at the end of a year they provide further evidence for reporting purposes. In terms of recording a teacher needs only to indicate when a piece has been selected so that at the end of the year there is an overview of how many pieces there are in the portfolio. This system is best used occasionally rather than systematically. There is no need, for example, to identify one piece per topic or unit. There may be two pieces of work in one unit which are thought to provide valuable evidence and none in others.

Some teachers are already using more sophisticated techniques for gathering and retaining evidence, and these can be used to supplement the examples we have given. For example, some teachers will tape-record conversations in the classroom; others have used film to record some of the classroom activities of pupils and some of their learning experiences outside school, such as visits. These can also form part of a more general record to amplify the picture of what pupils are doing in RE. Some Key Stage Four teachers are encouraging pupils to keep a personal diary in which they note and reflect on the development of their awareness of particular issues. This is kept by the pupil, shared with the teacher on occasions, and used to stimulate the reflective capacity of the pupils. Used with care, it can provide a basis for pupils to think about their own development.

There will always be some practical issues about who should hold or retain some of the evidence that is collected, in what form it should be retained, and for how long. These decisions are best made by individual teachers in line with school policy. Clearly the two situations which need to be avoided are, at the one extreme, where there are storage problems with the accumulation of great quantities of evidence, and at the other extreme, where evidence entrusted to pupils to retain for later reference becomes lost.

Reporting RE

As we have already suggested, reporting is a further distillation of what has been recorded. That is, teachers have to select from the recorded and gathered evidence over a period of time in order to present a more general and rounded picture of pupils' progress and development.

Reporting procedures in RE will clearly have to be in accordance with local policy. As this differs from school to school and between areas, these comments can only be of a general nature. We do, however, believe that there are two overriding values in the reporting process. These are:

1 To educate parents about what their children are doing in RE and what we are trying to achieve through RE.
2 To inform parents about their children's achievements so that they can be supportive partners in the learning process.

The first of these is just as important as the second. The regular flow of information to parents should help to draw them increasingly into an interest in and an awareness of what RE is about. Ideally, there should be three sources which contribute to this process, and they are described below.

The school's RE programme

These should be public documents which set out what RE aims to achieve and what pupils will be learning in RE. The school's curriculum statement should be broad and should tell parents and other interested parties about the kind of RE their children will be taught, its value to their overall broad and balanced education, and how it contributes to their development. It should in turn reflect what is said in the local authority's Agreed Syllabus of Religious Education, which has the same standing in law as the National Orders for the core and foundation subjects.

Parents should also be informed about the main elements of the school's programme for RE so that they are aware of the learning experiences and content of the subject. These should be based on and interpreted from any Programmes of Study which the LEA may include in its Agreed Syllabus or in non-statutory guidance. Even if the school's RE programme is not sent to all parents, it should still be in the form of a public document which is there for parents to see.

The pupil profile

The real value of the pupil profile is that it can serve these purposes:

- It provides a process by which pupils can monitor their own progress and reflect on their own ideas.
- It provides a record of evidence of achievement.
- It can provide a vehicle for reporting regularly to parents.

The third purpose can be met if pupils take home their profile form at the end of each substantial topic or unit for parents to see and initial. From this, parents can have an up-to-date picture both of what pupils have done in RE and of what they have achieved through it. They may not easily absorb the overview of RE contained in the school's curriculum statement or programme, but they can gain a quick impression from a regular profile of what is happening and what their children have gained from the experience. Many teachers have found that making time and space for this exercise has brought considerable rewards in terms of parental awareness and interest. The profile does not need to be elaborate or repetitive, but if it is used carefully, both pupils and parents can value it as a way of keeping each other informed.

The summative report

The emerging pattern of summative reporting is one in which schools report to parents at the end of the year and at the end of each Key Stage. This overall pattern is a process culminating in a summative record of achievement.

Reporting on RE should be parallel with other core and foundation subjects. However, it will be for local authorities to decide in what form this is to be done. We think it is highly unlikely that there will be any externally applied assessments, except those which relate to the much more narrowly defined GCSE in Religious Studies. All assessments will therefore be carried out by teachers and monitored by the LEA. We also believe that reporting in RE will be confined to the overall notion of 'RE' rather than to particular components within RE. There will therefore be no requirement to weigh Attainment Targets differentially where they exist in local documents or to aggregate results from those Attainment Targets.

Summative reporting in RE should be broadly based. It may refer to particular achievements of pupils. The summative and descriptive statements made by teachers will be supported by the evidence that has been gathered over the relevant period of time.

The process is not simply a question of leaving pupils to themselves to determine their own progress. It is a way of engaging pupils in a dialogue about their progress. The teacher continues to make observations and judgements, but the pupils participate and offer their own observations. It is a process which has particular value in RE. It is this self-monitoring element which is the most appropriate medium for carrying out those broad formative assessments relating to pupil development in the areas of sensitivities, patterns of awareness, personal qualities and attitudes, beliefs and values. These are central to RE.

PART SIX

Summary

We began in the first Part of this book with a statement of a general aim for Religious Education. From this aim and the examples of content indicated by the RE field of enquiry, we have set about showing how the subject can be planned, taught and assessed in both primary and secondary schools. It is hoped that teachers of RE will take from this manual all that will be of help when planning their own programme of RE in school. To assist them in this we summarise below some of the main points which have been developed in this manual.

It is the task of RE to ensure that children have gained some understanding of religion by the time they leave school; that they have explored something of the relationship between religious perspectives and wider human experiences; and that they have reflected for themselves on the relevance of these perspectives and experiences for their own beliefs, attitudes and behaviour.

(Part One)

The field of enquiry sets out the potential range of content which the subject may explore. It comprises three interrelated areas: traditional belief systems, shared human experience and individual patterns of belief. These are not separate static bodies of knowledge, but form a dynamic whole.

(Part Two)

The aim of the subject is achieved through the interaction of children with the teacher and content drawn from the RE field of enquiry.

(Part Three)

RE, like any other subject, depends on an understanding of the fact that teaching must be related to the ability of the children and their appropriate stage of development.

(Part Two)

When the logical structure of the RE field of enquiry is linked to insights into the ways in which children learn, a self-evident sequencing pattern emerges. RE begins with the observable features of religion and human experience and moves towards those abstract cores of beliefs, spirituality and ultimate questions.

The systems approach and life themes approach represent different ways of exploring the RE field of enquiry. Both approaches remain faithful to the essential nature of the subject, for they enable relevant links to be made between the three areas of the field of enquiry.

(Part Three)

Any topic that is chosen must have potential for exploring an aspect of the RE field of enquiry.

(Part Three)

The quality of teaching or the methods of directing pupil learning adopted by teachers are crucial if the subject matter is to come alive and be processed by pupils in a way which genuinely contributes to their learning.

(Part Four)

There is no one set pattern or sequence of activities for all RE lessons. Teachers should combine segments which motivate pupils and help them to explore and express faith responses.

(Part Four)

The problem of presumption may be overcome by altering patterns of the statements used by teachers of RE. It is possible to find ways of speaking which leave them free to state clearly what they believe, what this or that tradition believes and does, without denying to pupils the freedom to respond from their perspective.

(Part Four)

The nature of RE is such that it is less concerned with measuring individual gradings than with assessing the way in which children are learning (especially in interaction with each other) and with the benefits they are deriving from it in terms of personal growth and maturity.

(Part Five)

In itself this manual has been concerned as much with how to teach as it has been with what to teach and why it is taught. Supplementary manuals which accompany this general manual explore and explain in detail how and when to teach different aspects of the subject's field of enquiry. They also provide detailed scope and sequence charts related to each religion and to significant life themes. In this sense they complement and extend the principles and procedures outlined in this manual.

Bibliography

Barrat, M., Magnier, N., Rudge, J., Teece, G., *Attainment in RE – A Handbook for Teachers*, Regional RE Centre (Midlands), 1989

Cole, W. Owen (ed.), *World Faiths in Education*, George Allen and Unwin, 1978
    Religion in the Multifaith School, Hulton, 1983

Copley, Terence, *RE Being Served?*, CIO Publishers, 1985

Cox, Edwin, *Problems and Possibilities for Religious Education*, Hodder and Stoughton, 1983

Cox, E. and Cairns, J., *Reforming Religious Education*, Bedford Way Papers, Institute of Education, University of London, 1988

Gower, R., *Religious Education at the Primary Stage – A Handbook for Teachers and Governors*, Lion Education, 1990

Hertfordshire LEA, *Recognising Achievement in RE*, Hertfordshire County Council, 1991

Grimmit, Michael, *What Can I Do in RE?*, 2nd edn, Mayhew-McCrimmon, 1978
    Religious Education and Human Development, McCrimmon, 1987

Holley, Raymond, *Religious Education and Religious Understanding*, Routledge and Kegan Paul, 1978

Holm, Jean, *Teaching Religion in School*, Oxford University Press, 1975
    The Study of Religions, Sheldon Press, 1977

Hull, John, *School Worship – an Obituary*, SCM, 1975
    New directions in Religious Education, The Falmer Press, 1982
    Studies in Religion and Education, The Falmer Press, 1984
    The Act Unpacked, CEM, 1988
    God Talk with Young Children, CEM, 1990

Jackson, Robert (ed.), *Approaching World Religions*, John Murray, 1982

Jackson, R. and Starking, D. (eds), *The Junior RE Handbook*, Stanley Thornes, 1990

National Curriculum Council, *Religious Education: A Local Curriculum Framework*, 1991

O'Leary, D. J., and Sallow, T., *Love and Meaning in Religious Education*, Oxford University Press, 1982

Religious Education Council of England and Wales, *RE, Attainment and the National Curriculum*, 1991

Rodger, A. R., *Education and Faith in an Open Society*, The Handsel Press, 1982

Rudge, J., *Assessing, Recording and Reporting RE – A Handbook for Teachers*, Regional RE Centre (Midlands), 1991

Schools Council Working Paper 44, *RE in the Primary School*, Evans/Methuen Educational, 1972
    Working Paper 36, *RE in the Secondary School*, Evans/Methuen Educational, 1971
    Religious Education in Primary Schools: Discovering an Approach, Macmillan Educational, 1977

Sealey, John, *Religious Education: Philosophical Perspectives*, George Allen & Unwin, 1985

Smart, Ninian, *Secular Education and the Logic of Religion*, Faber and Faber, 1968

Smart, Ninian and Horder, Donald, *New Movements in RE*, Temple Smith, 1975

Sutcliffe, John M. (Ed.), *A Dictionary of Religious Education*, SCM, 1984

Tilby, Angela, *Teaching God*, Collins Fount Paperback, 1979

Watson, B., *Education and Belief*, Basil Blackwell, 1987

Index

THE WESTHILL PROJECT R E 5–16 is a comprehensive range of materials for teaching Religious Education in schools, from lower primary to upper secondary level.

Spanning the whole WESTHILL PROJECT the second edition of the teacher's manual **HOW DO I TEACH R E ?** provides comprehensive help with structuring an R E course, and can stand on its own as an excellent all-round guide to the teaching of R E.

- Explores the aims and structure of R E as a school subject, and how these can be translated into classroom practice.
- Gives clear guidance for school-based syllabus planning and curriculum development.
- Maintains a continuity of approach from the earlier edition.
- Incorporates much new thinking about the R E curriculum, particularly in relation to attainment and assessment.
- Reflects the broad consensus evident in the most up-to-date of the local education authority agreed syllabuses.

Project materials are available on some of the major world religions, and on the **Life Themes** strand to the project, with others in preparation.

Series Editors are staff of the Regional R E Centre (Midlands), Westhill College, Birmingham.

Stanley Thornes

Old Station Drive
Leckhampton
CHELTENHAM
Glos. GL53 0DN

ISBN 0-7487-1470-7

9 780748 714704